Byambasuren Davaa was born in the year of the pig in Ulaanbaatar and moved to Germany in 1999 to study at the Munich Academy of Television and Film. Her previous film, *The Story of the Weeping Camel*, was a surprise hit with critics and audiences across the world and was shown in over thirty countries, winning an Oscar nomination for best documentary. As a child, Davaa stayed in her grandmother's ger and experienced the nomadic way of life portrayed in this book.

Lisa Reisch was born in Marburg in 1978, studied Ethnography at Munich's Ludwig Maximilian University and Documentary Filmmaking at the Munich Academy of Television and Film. She was assistant director on *The Cave of the Yellow Dog* and worked closely with Byambasuren Davaa on this book.

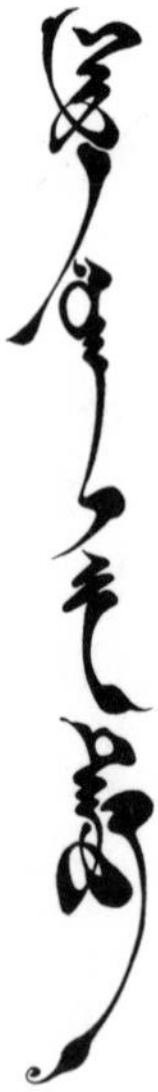

The Cave of the Yellow Dog

A Mongolian Journey

Byambasuren Davaa and Lisa Reisch

Translated by Sally-Ann Spencer

virago

Inspired by a story by Gantuya Lhagva

VIRAGO

Published in Germany in 2005 by Piper Verlag GmbH, München
First published in Great Britain in 2007 by Virago Press

Photographs reproduced by kind permission of
Monika Höfler and Daniel Schönauer.

Calligraphic illustrations by Battomor Dashbaldan.

A CIP catalogue record for this book
is available from the British Library.

ISBN 978-1-84408-304-6

Typeset in Goudy by M Rules
Printed and bound in Great Britain by
Clays Ltd, St Ives plc

Virago Press
An imprint of
Little, Brown Book Group
Brettenham House
Lancaster Place
London WC2E 7EN

A Member of the Hachette Group of Companies

www.virago.co.uk

'There are many stories within me. Inside everyone there are stories unfurling like seeds, preparing to bloom. Now the time has come to tell of *The Cave of the Yellow Dog*.'

Byambasuren Davaa

Foreword

I left Mongolia in the winter of 1999 to apply for a place at the Munich Academy of Television and Film.

I returned in the spring of 2004 on a research trip for my graduation film. The inspiration for the film and, later, this book came from a Mongolian fable, *The Cave of the Yellow Dog*. In this book, my friend and assistant director Lisa Reisch and I place the story in context and explore my culture from a European vantage point, looking at Mongolia and the nomadic tradition from an outsider's perspective. Our obser-vations and reflections form the basis of a series of short pieces on such topics as food, music, politics and domestic life.

Before moving to Germany I had no experience of living abroad. In the course of a single trip I found myself separated from my homeland by thousands of kilometres. The flight from Ulaanbaatar, the Mongolian capital, to Frankfurt via Berlin took fourteen hours. When my partner Batbayar and I arrived in the German capital, I was loath to step out of the plane.

The next stop, Frankfurt airport, was a monolith of con-crete and glass. The airport clock read half past five in the afternoon, but a glance at my wrist showed the day had ended half an hour ago. Bagy re-set his watch.

We struggled through the terminal buildings with our heavy bags. A steady stream of incomprehensible announce-ments reverberated through the halls, accompanying our slow progress. Glass kiosks extended into the distance while music played overhead. The towering ceilings were unlike anything I had ever seen. Not a hint of clear skies.

A tunnel inside the airport took us on a journey that seemed to last for ever. It was not yet evening, but darkness had already fallen. Tiny drops of water shimmered on the hair and shoulders of the people coming towards us. It must have been raining or snowing outside. Old ladies were braving the elements in sheer tights. I felt a chill on the inside. That morning the temperature in my homeland had sunk to thirty degrees below zero.

The people around us wore plain, dark clothes. I saw young women hurry past in black jackets, black trousers and black shoes with thick raised soles.

There were policemen everywhere.

A stranger approached Batbayar in the railway station. Bagy had studied for a while in the former GDR at Dresden University, but this was the first time I had heard him speak German. Despite attending six months of German classes in Ulaanbaatar, I understood nothing of what he said. I felt discouraged and nervous. Would I ever be able to cope here? Bagy was going back to Mongolia in four weeks and I was apprehensive about staying on alone.

According to the stranger, there was a cheaper way of getting to Munich. Since any means of saving money was welcome, we decided to buy his tickets, at a tenth of the standard fare. For the time being I stopped worrying about whether we could afford to live in Germany. The man led us on to the platform and introduced us to two foreigners – Egyptians, I think. Bagy took care of the negotiations, paid the money and took possession of our bargain tickets.

Later we realised why the strangers were able to give us such a remarkable deal: unstamped tickets could be purchased for five marks from passengers leaving the train. We had paid fifteen marks for two. Is this how the free market economy works? I wondered. Seven-and-a-half marks per person to travel five hundred kilometres each – not a bad price. The knowledge that prices were negotiable in this strange and unknown land went some way towards allaying my fears.

We climbed on and found ourselves a seat. At last we were off. I pressed my face to the window and saw coloured streaks of flickering light. It was silent in the compartment. Our fellow passengers sat with their backs pressed against their seats, most of them reading.

At that moment a door opened. A man in a dark blue suit and cap walked in and shouted something incomprehensible. Passengers who, only seconds earlier, had been buried in their books and magazines sprang into life. The man in the suit and cap made his way down the right-hand side of the carriage, saying a few words to each passenger and holding out his hand. With a flash of teeth he took the outstretched ticket. He punched it with a hand-held instrument and returned it to its owner. His features returned to their natural arrangement, teeth retreating behind his lips.

What could it mean?

The man turned round and repeated the ritual on the left-hand side of the carriage. Slowly I began to understand. When it came to me, I smiled as he showed me his teeth and ventured a tentative *danke*.

A few hours later, when Bagy and I had witnessed five or so variations of the same ritual, I understood how it was that 'good journeys' and 'happy weekends' were dispensed with such ease. Worn out by the effort of changing trains, I dropped into yet another seat, opened my bottle of water and took a big gulp. The carbonated water tickled my throat, bubbles exploding in my nose. I was on the brink of tears. Was this another bargain like the ticket? I checked with Bagy. When I learned that the bottle cost three marks, I did the sums in my head. One bottle of German water was worth two thousand tugrik, which meant that my entire monthly salary came to fifty litres of German water.

I was tired, weighed down by the time difference. Caught between two nights I longed for dawn.

I spent my first night in Germany in the waiting room at Munich station. My watch showed twenty past seven in the morning, but the station clock read 00.20. I re-set my watch and closed my eyes until I was running barefoot across a flow-ered carpet of never-ending steppe. Thunder rolled above me and it started to rain. I surveyed my surroundings. There was no one but me. Turning back, I felt a pinprick in my sole. I looked down. A shard of glass. I pulled it out and cast it away. Shards of glass in a myriad of colours. A moment ago things had been so different. I felt like crying but had no tears and no voice.

As I woke, dawn light was streaming through the window of the waiting room.

The Cave of the Yellow Dog

Preface

White lake of Djirim
Your water sinks from year to year.
Mother of great children
You get smaller by the year.
Waiting mother
The stars and moon are your solace.

MONGOLIAN FOLK SONG

I am on my way home, returning to the place where my mother was born.

The search for a family for my graduation film takes me to the province of Arkhanghai, in north-west Mongolia. We drive for two days from Ulaanbaatar through the barren prairie landscape towards the north-west.

I meet many people on the way and draw inspiration from them all, but am yet to find a girl who is capable of carrying the story. I also need a small child, a toddler who will play a central role. Finding the right family takes far longer than expected. According to the dashboard, our Russian SUV has already notched up 3620 kilometres. Will my search be rewarded? Doubts set in.

In the crater landscape of the white lake I come across the spring camp of Buyandulam, Batchuluun and their three children. After the official greeting, a ritual conducted courteously and warmly in all households, we get to know each other better.

The mother, Buyandulam, or Buena for short, apologises for the state of their camp. The family practises otor – always on the move to find the best grazing. After the cold winter months vegetation is still sparse and families can find themselves changing camp each week in search of fresh pastures. Their households are run on a makeshift basis.

Unlike Batchuluun, who comes from a long line of nomads, Buena grew up in the province's township, the child of an urban family. Batchuluun says little but laughs a good deal, his eyes disappearing behind his sharply drawn features. While he grooms the goats, I ask him about the financial pressures on nomadic families.

Batchuluun and his wife are in their early thirties. Together they are responsible for three hundred animals and three children. As is customary in Mongolia, the children talk to each other using the familiar form of address, but use the formal form to speak to their parents. At one-and-a-half years old, Batbayar, the youngest child, is extremely inquisitive. He starts to dance as soon as his sister, four-year-old Nansalmaa, sings a welcome song in our honour. Thrilled by the younger children's artlessness, I wait nervously for the eldest daughter to appear. She is outside with the animals but returns before long to the ger, their traditional felt-clad tent.

Six-year-old Nansaa is the image of her father. At first she ignores me pointedly, responding with one-word answers when I try to get her talking. I hope to excite her interest with my digital camera, but she looks at the photos from a distance. At last, when the talk turns to animals, we gradually build a rapport. I am impressed by her confident, knowledgeable and perceptive comments about an injured calf.

Nansaa is the headstrong girl who will take my viewers on their journey through the film. She is also the main character in this book, joining us on our travels through rural Mongolia.

I had to resist the temptation to ask the family there and then whether they would allow me and a German film crew to spend the summer with them. We needed more time to get to know each other first. I asked permission to return the next day.

Without knowing how Buena and Batchuluun would react to my proposal, I returned to the province township, a modern nomad on the move between two worlds, separated from my German home by a fourteen-hour flight.

1

'Everyone dies, but no one is dead.'

A man walks, blue skies above, grey earth below, bearing the body of a dog. His daughter follows behind. Uncomplaining, the rugged hillside accepts the lowered corpse, a body without a soul. A sharp knife slices deftly through the tail.

'What are you doing?' asks the child.

'The tail belongs under the head. That way the dog will be reborn as a man with a ponytail and not an animal with a tail. See the butter in his mouth? That will be his first meal.'

Father and daughter entrust the body of the dog to the care of the mountain.

2

The wind, tired of sweeping the steppe since daybreak, comes to rest in the mountaintops. Another summer's night draws in. After a hot day grazing on the plains the sheep are weary too. Their unshorn coats seek the coolness of the barren, stony ground.

As the moon rises, the son of night will show his face. Howling, he announces his arrival. By day he gathers his strength; at night he sings his warning from the mountain.

His howls stir the sleeping valley. The sheep rise nervously to their feet, snorting as his followers answer. Newborn lambs call out in bewilderment, their cries faltering in the darkness. The flock chases back and forth in panic. There is a clamour of bleats and a clattering of horns. The pack of wolves draws closer, approaching from every angle.

Batchuluun comes running from the ger. Armed only with shrieks and piercing cries he must override his fear.

The dull metallic thump of the ladle striking wood will scare away the wolves. Buena rushes after her husband, shouting and drumming with all her might, knowing that one sheep has already been taken.

The individual notes of their voices are lost in the cacophony.

'Now I've broken the ladle!' cries Buena. Her voice is surprisingly powerful, the sound of a woman who is used to defending her camp against the prowling sovereign of the steppe.

Batchuluun stumbles over a second corpse while trying to herd the scattered animals in the darkness. His shouts, cast back by the rocks, reverberate through the valley. The wolves stop their howling.

*

The wind, age-old witness of time, sees the passing of many things; tomorrow it will sweep away another story.

3

The grass, by night a cradle for the animals, tilts up towards the dawn. Two white gers, one large, one small, stand beside a little lake. A vertical column of smoke rises calmly from the stove-pipe protruding from one of the tents, and merges with the thin wisps of cloud.

A noise gathers in the distance; it seems out of place in these surroundings. At the sound of the roaring motor, Buena breaks off her morning libations. Clad in her lilac summer deel, the traditional Mongolian robe, and with a yellow sash tied loosely at her waist, she hurries out to the dead sheep. The night of terror is reflected in their staring eyes. She tries to close them, but they reopen, the muscles in the eyelids already rigid.

'Batchuluun, come quickly!'

With the help of her husband she carries the savaged sheep to the grass behind the tent. Her movements are deft and assured. Her hair is pulled back from her face in a plait.

The truck is already in sight. Buena gathers the broken ladle abandoned last night on the awning and places it in the ger. Batchuluun covers the dead animals with a sack. He must hurry for he can already hear the car door slamming.

He listens as Buena gives a warm welcome to the driver, whose job it is to bring the school children home to their scattered families on the steppe. Today is their eldest daughter's homecoming.

4

Still in her school uniform, cheeks tanned by the wind and sun, Nansaa sips her mother's milk tea. This is the moment she has been waiting for.

Before school started, she had never really been away from home. Now the ger seems special. The shrine is in its usual place on the sacred side of the tent, a pan of milk, fresh that morning, simmers on the stove, and her father's tools are stored, as always, on the right-hand side of the tent.

Her little sister Nansalmaa and baby brother Batbayar are asleep.

Nothing has changed in her weeks of absence. She can relax. This is home.

Buena fetches Nansaa's deel from the wardrobe. 'See how you've grown. You'll be able to tether the one-horned cow's stubborn little calf all by yourself.'

Rather than answering her parents' questions about her stay in the city, Nansaa wants a full report on all that has happened at home.

'Did Nansalmaa take good care of Batbayar? What about the injured kid? Is it better? Did you make lots of milk vodka? Did the wolves come back?'

'Yes,' Batchuluun says reticently.

Nansaa starts to ask if the wolves killed lots of sheep. 'Drink your tea before it gets cold,' interrupts her mother.

'Why don't you show me your schoolbooks?' her father suggests.

Brimming with pride, Nansaa shows off the stars she was given for good work.

School

'Open up, oh golden gate,' cried the Prince.
If it opens to the side, you will step in without a care.
If it opens from the top or bottom it will cast you into the
air or squash you to the ground.
But if you learn your lessons, little Prince, you will come to
know the workings of the hinge.

BAABAR (BAT-ERDENE BATBAYER),
Mongolian politician and writer

In my case, starting school marked the end of a magical age, presided over by my grandmother and her stories. I soon came to learn that the age of fairy tales is not an enduring one and comes abruptly and painfully to an end.

Since my parents both left for work each morning before I got up, I went to school with uncombed hair. Comb and ribbon in hand, my exasperated teacher would plait my hair, a task that had been performed by my grandmother before she passed away.

I loved my school uniform. By putting it on each morning I took on a specific yet universal role, happy at being a girl among many. I never felt envious or wanted to compete, unlike my niece who goes to school without a uniform and is more individualistic.

When I was a pupil in the late 1970s and early 1980s illiteracy was almost unheard of in Mongolia. By 1989, on the eve of democracy, Mongolia had achieved a literacy rate of almost 100 per cent, a notable achievement given its nomadic population.

The Mongolian school system is based on the Russian model, which caters for children from nomadic families. These days compulsory schooling begins at the age of six or seven. Since most schools are located in urban centres, it used to be customary for nomadic children to wait until the age of nine or ten. Even now the distances are too great to be covered regularly, so the majority of children are unable to live at home. Young nomads find it just as hard as other children to be separated from their parents. Those families that can, lodge their children with relatives, a more popular option than enrolling them as boarders at the school.

The state provides free schooling, but the cost of boarding is borne by the parents. Most families use goods such as animals, meat or raw materials to settle a proportion of the bill. When I was a child, rural children were allocated an extra four-week break in March as well as the usual summer holidays from June to September. Nomadic families need their children to help out at home during the birthing season in the spring.

There were no grammar schools when I was growing up; everyone received the same basic education. Children attended primary school for three years, middle grade for three years and senior grade for two years. Pupils intending to enrol at Ulaanbaatar University spent a further two years in secondary education. To study in Germany I was required to attend university in Mongolia for a minimum of two years, so that the length of my education equalled that of prospective German students.

The past fifteen years have seen the emergence of private schools based on Western models – the French lycée, the American high school, the German grammar school – but the basic Mongolian state system remains unchanged.

My first day at school marked the start of a new chapter in my life, during which I would spend all my afternoons until middle grade in the classroom. Our lessons ran from one in the afternoon until six in the evening. The older children were taught in the mornings.

Since my teacher had made it clear that plaiting my hair was not her responsibility, my father decided to cut it off. The unceremonious loss of my plait – my talisman against evil spirits – was something my grandmother would never have allowed.

The last vestiges of my belief in fairy tales fell away with my locks.

Family photo: *from left*, Batbayar, Batchuluun, Nansalmaa, Nansaa and Buena.

The Batchuluun family
and film crew.

Top: Zochor; more of a troublemaker than a sheepdog.

Middle: Cinematographer Daniel Schönauer and Director Byambasuren Davaa.

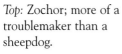

Bottom: Lisa Reisch with six-year-old Nansaa.

Overleaf: hunting for treasure in the sky.

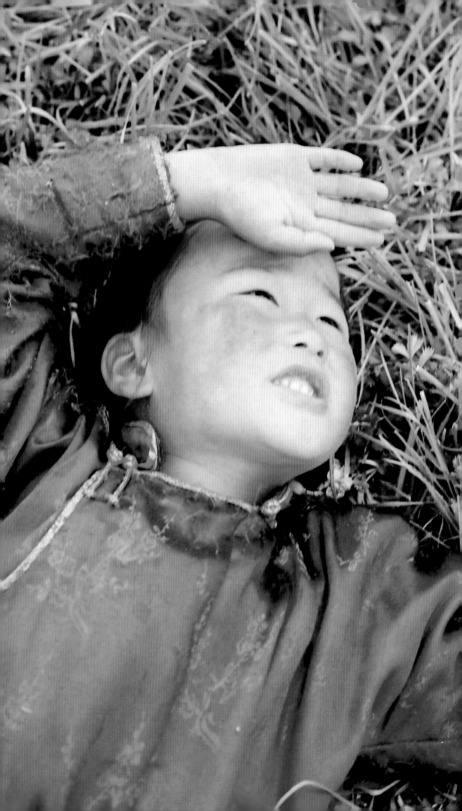

Batchuluun and
Buena, both in their
early thirties, have
three children and
three hundred animals
in their care.
Batchuluun is a nomad
by birth, while Buena
grew up in the
province capital, the
child of an urban
family.

Byambasuren Davaa with Zochor, the 'Coloured One', and his doppelgänger.

5

School in the sum township was fun, but Nansaa is glad to be home with her family. Her sister is wide-eyed with astonishment at her tales of the faraway place.

One day after Nansaa's return to the summer camp, she and her siblings are playing with dung. Usually they arrange the patties into miniature gers but this time Nansaa piles them high, stacking the tower as tall as she can.

'I'd live up high if we lived in the city,' she says. 'It's too dark down below.'

An imaginary town, inspired by Nansaa's stories, takes shape in Nansalmaa's mind. Rivers run through the felt-clad walls of the ger, water gushing into waiting pans. The streets are full of people, more than at her grandparents' New Year celebrations, and milk is drunk from little paper buckets. Animals are scarce.

A basket of twigs is requisitioned as a bus. Baby Batbayar must play the schoolboy while Nansalmaa takes the wheel.

'Why don't you fetch some dung instead of playing?' Buena says to Nansaa.

For the first time ever Nansaa is dispatched on her own to look for fuel. Hoisting the bus to her shoulders, she sets off with a pitch fork. She must use the prongs to scoop up the cakes of dried dung and fling them deftly into the basket on her back. If only her father could see her now. She swells with pride.

Batchuluun has been gone since first thing that morning. The flock moves fastest in the fresh dawn air. In recent years the winters have been more bleak than ever and the extremely arid summers have taken the nomads by surprise. Batchuluun must travel further afield if the grassland around the camp is to be spared for harsher times.

He guides the animals to a natural spring. The sheep are still drinking thirstily when two riders, guns and binoculars slung over their shoulders, cross the stream.

Glad of the unexpected company, Batchuluun greets the two men. Encounters with hunters are increasingly rare. The elder of the pair, Hunter Sharaw, is a shrewd and experienced man. Laughter lines crease his tanned face, the traces of a thousand stories. The younger man is at pains not to give his friend more cause than usual to poke fun at his expense.

'And the hunting? How is it this summer?'

Bottles of snuff pass from hand to hand and news is exchanged. Batchuluun laughs. He has no desire to be hawked around the countryside in one of this old hunter's stories. Sharaw gleefully recounts how he waited for the younger man that morning and eventually found him on his hands and knees beside the lake. The best way of washing the vodka from his belly was to push him into the water, which Sharaw promptly did.

His companion cleans his gun sheepishly. He already knows his fate. Over the next few days he will stand and listen as last night's exploits turn into a wild adventure, whose fanciful embellishments his mother will quote back to him at home.

Sharaw switches topics: 'Is the area peaceful here?'

'We've lost another two sheep to the wolf,' says Batchuluun.

'No one joins together to drive them out like we used to. They're all moving to the city. Times are good for the predator in grey.'

'I'll have to drive to the city tomorrow to sell the sheep-skins.'

Batchuluun's sheep have drunk their fill by the time the hunters mount their horses. Before they depart, Sharaw asks a favour: 'Could you pick up some ammunition from Badam's shop for me?' Batchuluun is happy to help out.

Up and down, Nansaa plods determinedly over the bumpy terrain of the steppe. Pats of dung lie all around her, but Nansaa's inexperience shows. She knows she must lift the pats and cast them behind her, but how can she tell where the basket is and how much momentum is required? With each attempt the dung shoots past the basket or soars upwards and lands on her head.

Spinning round to see behind her, Nansaa turns in circles like a kid goat with a stinging nettle in its mouth. No matter how hard she tries, the crumbling pats refuse to co-operate. Nansaa perseveres. Intent on mastering her difficult task she wanders further and further away from camp.

After a while the ground changes beneath her feet. The earth becomes stonier, the dry pats fewer and farther between.

'Nearly tripped and died,' mutters Nansaa, steadying her-self after stumbling over another big stone. By now her legs weigh as heavily as the empty basket pulling on her back. At last she glances back and, realising that the ger is masked by hills, flops down on a boulder in exhaustion.

The valley has narrowed and the rock face looms above

her. With the sun at its zenith, there is no shade to be had in the gorge. Chirping crickets are the only creatures that dance and make music in such heat. Or perhaps they are singing in protest, invoking the wind against the fierce sun.

The medley of chirps is interrupted by a growl from the cliff. Nansaa listens intently. Looking round, she notices for the first time that the base of the rock is covered in bleached bones. Scattered sections of skeleton – horses' skulls, goats' jawbones, sheep's anklebones – litter the ground at her feet.

With the curiosity of a fearless young marmot, Nansaa approaches the towering wall of rock. Guided by growls and whimpers she finds herself at the opening of a cave.

She barely hesitates, peering bravely inside the black hole gaping in the rock. Startled legs scamper back and forth, not far away. She clambers inside.

'Who's there?' she calls. The crickets appeal forlornly to the wind. 'What's your name?' whispers Nansaa. 'Haven't you got a mother?' She thinks for a moment. 'You can come home with me.'

The cave releases a pup from the darkness. 'Don't run away, boy! Here, drink this.' Nansaa spits on her hand and lets the little dog lick it. 'That's settled then,' she tells it. 'You and I are friends and your new name is Zochor.'

Outside the cave the dog chases its tail in confusion. Snarling and snapping it defies the girl's commands. Nansaa calls it by its new name but the puppy ignores her. 'Here boy!' She won't go home empty-handed after all.

6

Frothing, the bubbles subside in the tub. Buena adds more water before the suds can settle. Her hands resume their practised rhythm – soap, fabric, scouring – the routine of scrubbing clothes. The water billows with foam.

A pair of trousers demands Batbayar's full attention. He lays them flat on the grass to dry, but they insist on folding in on themselves. Frowning in concentration he throws a few clumsy stones to pin the fabric down. He must not allow the wind to sweep his trousers into the stream.

Nansaa, empty basket slung across her back, heads towards him from the other bank. In one hand she holds the pitchfork, in the other her sash. Like an extension of her arm, it loops around the dog's neck, tying the two friends together. She makes her way across the stream, teetering over the water that swirls between the stepping stones. She fights to keep her balance as the young dog strains at the leash. Her concentration falters. In an instant the puppy has broken free and is hurtling towards Buena.

'Who's this you've brought home with you? Has the dung grown legs?'

Nansaa fidgets, trying to think of what to say. For now she is saved by Nansalmaa, who comes running from the ger and starts playing with the pup.

'I expect his owners will be looking for him,' Buena comments. 'They must have lost him when they moved.'

'He was in a cave all by himself, Mother! And anyway, he already knows his name!' Buena listens while her daughter explains that she called him Zochor, meaning 'coloured one', because of his spots. The children don't notice their mother's misgivings.

7

Batchuluun sits on the floor of the ger, sharpening his knife. He must skin the dead sheep before evening if he wants to find a buyer for the fleece. The wolves have cost him enough already without his family losing out again.

For once he has made up his mind not to sprinkle the skins with salt to preserve them. Normally he would wait for an itinerant trader to pass by and exchange the tanned skins for other goods – matches, salt, candles, flour or rice. This time

Batchuluun wants to take the skins to the city and sell them himself. These days he has a reasonable hope of making a profitable sale and the journey is less daunting now that he has a new motorcycle.

Dorj, his brother, left the steppe a year ago, but only after wolf attacks and climate swings had cost him half of his herd. The other half he sold, so as not to end up like other nomadic families who arrived in the city empty-handed, despite their hard work. Now Dorj is a trader in Ulaanbaatar, buying and selling wares he once produced – milk, meat and wool.

Batchuluun has learned from his brother that middlemen buy up skins, cashmere and wool and sell them to factories in the capital, who then send the goods abroad. A long line of people are waiting to make a living from his sheep. Dorj will offer him the best price for his wares.

In the past, Batchuluun has always declined his brother's offer to be a partner in the business, but now he is beset with doubts about his future as a nomad.

He tests the blade on his thumb. He inherited the knife from his grandfather and the metal has worn thin.

Zochor comes bounding into the ger, scattering his thoughts. 'Nansaa, come here this minute! Take the dog away, do you hear?' At the end of a long day's herding, Batchuluun is none too pleased to see his daughter's find. Now his patience snaps. His voice is raised to a shout. With his large weather-beaten hands he seizes the pup by the neck and pushes it roughly out of the ger.

'You can bet that dog lived with wolves.'

'There weren't any wolves where I found him!' Nansaa contradicts him.

'Caves are for wolves, not dogs.'

Nansaa stops crouching stubbornly by the door and darts after Zochor. Her dog is frightened and she will have to win him back.

Buena, returning to the ger after washing the dishes, is taken aback by her husband's resolve. 'You should have said no from the beginning,' he reproaches her. 'If Nansaa had returned the dog right away, we wouldn't be in this trouble now.'

'You know how she is. If her heart is set on something, it's hard to change her mind.'

Batchuluun straightens his back. All this crouching has sent his legs to sleep. He uses the grindstone to prise the boot from his foot, allowing the blood to flow back to his calf.

'What if we let it stay? Perhaps it was meant to be,' says Buena.

Batchuluun gets to his feet. In his opinion, stray dogs are worse than wolves. People don't appreciate how dangerous they are. And with so many families moving to the city, their numbers are increasing because the dogs get left behind. Wild dogs have no respect for humans.

'I've heard stories of stray dogs attracting wolves to the ger.

At least a wolf knows its boundaries. You don't see wolves filling their bellies by daylight.' Batchuluun wipes the sharp
blade across the rough fabric of his deel. The knife is ready
for use.

8

The sheepskins are laid out on the grass outside the ger. Animal fat clings to Batchuluun's knife. Zochor bounds up and licks the blanket of hide that Batchuluun has slipped between the skinless bodies and the steppe.

Batchuluun walks around the lake to the far side of a hill. The children would stumble upon the skinned corpses if he left them close to camp. Boggy earth gurgles greedily at his feet. Nature will decide who shall profit from the meat.

Batchuluun lights his pipe. Crows, gulls and eagles flock to the corpses faster than usual. Vultures circle menacingly overhead in the violet evening sky. The valley echoes with their raucous cries.

Animals

'The poor foreigner,' he said, 'has been acquainted with
our grasslands but for four short days.'
'We must pity him,' said the old man with feeling.
'How hard it must be,' commented the woman, 'not to be
born a Mongolian.'
'To be sure,' said the old man, 'the fellow is most unfortunate.
But how blessed he is to have found his way to us!'

FRITZ MÜHLENWEG, German painter and writer

35

It is winter 1999 and I am sitting in on my first classes at the Munich Academy of Television and Film. During a seminar on TV journalism a lecturer decides to screen a clip from a film about Mongolia. He introduces me to the class and I come under the scrutiny of inquisitive grey eyes.

He fast-forwards through the beginning of the film: camels, a desert landscape and a white ger hurtle across the screen. The sun rises in double time and the lecturer pauses the tape. The film continues at normal speed. We watch a detailed documentary about the slaughtering of a sheep.

One after the other the majority of the female students leave the room. Only a few men stay behind. My German is shaky and I miss much of what is said. It seems my fellow students are shocked by the images, which for me are a normal and natural part of nomadic existence. I feel more out of place than ever.

I think that was the moment when I first became aware of the gulf in our approach to death. For me and everyone watching the film, the culture of my ancestors, the tradition of slaughtering animals, assumed a new importance.

Did they find me distasteful in some way too?

Out of context, the act of slaughter provoked an extreme reaction among some of my fellow students. The nomad seized the sheep by its legs, laid it on its back and slit open its belly with a knife. That is the image that will have imprinted itself on many viewers' minds.

When I think about Mongolia and how animals are killed there, I remember my uncle, who would allow his sheep to gaze up at Father Sky before they died. My great-grandfather and his forefathers did the same. The slaughtered animal dies with dignity, for all living creatures are precious. Afterwards a butter lamp is lit as a reminder of the sacrifice of life.

We never slaughter lambs or calves, only fully grown animals chosen carefully from the flock. If an animal is killed by a wolf, we don't eat the flesh because its last waking moments were filled with suffering and fear. The blood of a slaughtered animal must never be spilt on Mother Earth.

Not long after the incident in the seminar I see a television documentary about slaughterhouse techniques in Germany. After a good deal of hesitation I resolve to watch the programme to the end. I want to understand the country that has become my new home.

The condemned pigs are squeezed head-to-tail in a holding pen. A blow is delivered to the forehead with an electric prod. The animals hit the dirt floor heavily, hooves protruding through the iron railings of the pen. Not a drop of blood. No knives. No intestines. Nothing. Clad in white protective suits, the men in charge of the deaths remind me of the first Mongolian astronaut who entered space in 1981.

Not for the first time, I feel like an alien in my new home.

I study the pictures from the abattoir, examining the

footage for evidence of a conscious effort to face up to the animals' death. I find none.

I watch other documentaries about life in Mongolia, hunting for television programmes and films about my country. I look in film archives and video shops but soon give up the trail. The footage is all too predictable. Almost every film or documentary culminates in the slaughter of a sheep.

I am more determined than ever to pass the entrance exam for the film academy. I want the Mongolians in my films to speak and tell their tale. This is my opportunity to show people in this country the diversity of my culture.

9

The sheep and goats bleat impatiently. In mild weather they usually spend the night on the steppe, but last night Batchuluun, anxious to protect them from attack, locked them in a pen. The flock waits for dawn, eager to start the day ahead.

Zochor sits in a forest of sheep and goat legs. His black-and-white coat is hard to spot among the milling bodies. He has been there since nightfall when Nansaa tied him to the pen to hide him from her father. Zochor resisted, growling at her and straining at the rope. When the sheep closed in and sniffed at the little intruder, he batted them away with one paw. A bad-tempered kid tried to charge him. Young horns twitching, it searched for contact with his flank. Zochor cowered, frightened and whimpering, beside the wooden post.

Now a strong hand unties the leash and sets him free. 'Tell Nansaa to take the dog back. I want him gone by the time I'm home.' Batchuluun lashes the sheepskins to his motorcycle.

'I'll talk to her,' says Buena. 'Could you get me a new ladle from town?'

'Is there anything else we need?'

'We should wait until after the move before we get more rice and flour.' Buena passes him the hat that he wears on special occasions.

'Yes, we'll get ready to break camp when I'm back.'

His time behind bars forgotten already, Zochor nibbles at the skins draped over the saddlebags. Batchuluun starts the engine with a kick and the bike roars into action. The dog leaps away.

'Look after yourselves,' shouts Batchuluun.

'Have a safe journey!'

Buena dips a cup into a wooden bucket and scatters yak's milk on the wind. The libation is for her husband, whose motorcycle moves slowly along the river valley towards the horizon: an offering for his safe return.

With the children still asleep, Buena performs her morning rituals undisturbed. Kneeling in front of the shrine, she gives thanks for the new sunrise. She recites her mantras in a low voice: 'Om mani padme hum'. Once, twice, thrice, she twists the wick of the butter lamp between her fingers. The direction is determined by the movement of the sun.

Bolstered by Buena's prayers, the wick points upwards from the centre of a small brass dish. Molten butter is poured on top, filling the dish with rising warmth. Buena lights the lamp and fills a second brass dish with milk.

Sunshine streams through the opening in the roof as if to soak up the offering. A plump fly weaves around the wooden struts, its green body shimmering in the light, before settling impudently on Batbayar's face. It has tracked down the remnants of yesterday's meal.

Batbayar wakes up. The door of the ger is open and a yak is suckling its calf. The calves have waited until Buena has finished milking to quench their thirst. Batbayar is thirsty too but he won't get a drink unless he wakes his sisters. Once they are up, they will bundle him down to the stream and scrub his face with icy water. Then comes a greater indignity: his hair will be scraped into two tight plaits. He hates it when they do that.

Batbayar needs a drink.

Hair

I stroke your long braids – but still I want more.
I press myself against your beautiful body – but still I want
more.
Were you born to win my love?
Does the beauty of Mongolian women make you more
beautiful still?

MONGOLIAN FOLK SONG

'Film sister,' Nansaa said to me one day while plaiting Lisa's hair, 'this poor woman has barely ten strands of hair on her head.' In the Mongolian steppe, wearing your hair down is a sign of loose morals. Like most places in the world, hair bears a special significance in Mongolian culture.

A child must reach a certain age before his or her hair may be cut. Children are thought to enter the world as flawless beings, so we strive to protect their natural perfection as long as we can. The custom probably originated in Mongolia's high rate of infant mortality. Tradition dictates that children wear their hair in two plaits: girls until they are four and boys until the age of three. It is hard to distinguish between boys and girls as a result.

Age is calculated differently in Mongolia compared to the West. The first nine months in the womb represent the initial year of life and are referred to as the 'empty year'.

The position of the stars determines the date of the hair-cutting ceremony, which marks the loss of the child's plaits and its official start in life. Ceremonies take place at odd-numbered ages for boys, usually when they are three or five.

During the ceremony the child stands in the middle of the room, dressed in his best deel and holding a pair of scissors and a khadag, a sacred blue scarf. The family elder or guest of honour is the first to use the scissors. His star-sign should harmonise with that of the child. He cuts a lock of hair, says a blessing and gives the child a present. The other family members follow suit.

Each guest snips a small lock of hair, which is placed in the khadag. In pastoral families the gifts take the form of young animals such as lambs, foals or kids.

At the end of the ceremony the parents shave the child's head. A lock of hair on an otherwise shorn head indicates that a significant family member was absent.

I remember my older brother telling me proudly about his big day. 'The most important person in the room was me,' he said.

He received more presents that day as a five-year-old than ever before or since.

There is a symbolism to cutting one's hair in old age too. Elderly people cut their hair in readiness for death. From that moment on they will live without sin: never killing another animal, eating meat, drinking alcohol or having sex.

For many Mongolians hair is not merely an indicator of social status or beliefs. The lunar calendar, which is still widely followed in Mongolia, prescribes the correct time for cutting your hair. A person's spirit migrates around the body, residing in different organs according to the position of the moon. On certain days it settles in the belly, on others in the liver, heart or head. If I followed the lunar calendar I would be sure to avoid the hairdresser when my spirit was in my head.

10

Nansaa hands the comb to her younger sister. Batbayar's braids are the least of her concerns.

'Mother, I hid Zochor from Father yesterday and now he's escaped from the sheep pen!'

'Hiding him won't help, you know,' says Buena, lifting the axle of the ox-cart.

A cheese is pinned beneath the solid wooden wheel. It looks ripe and ready for slicing.

'Quick, pull it out!' Buena instructs her daughter.

Nansaa darts forward. She knows her mother won't be able to bear the weight of the cart for long.

'The puppy's still here, little one, but you'll have to take him back today.'

'He's mine now,' Nansaa says truculently.

Buena lifts out the freshly pressed white cheese from its linen wrapping. 'It's turned out nicely.'

Nansaa crouches on the grass. As her mother slices off thin strips of cheese with a thread, she collects them and lays them on a wooden board to dry. Every now and then she glances up from her work and tries to spot Zochor.

'You understand why we can't keep him, don't you?' Buena asks her. She knows how stubborn her daughter can be.

'I know, I know. But Zochor isn't a wolf!'

'What if he lived with wolves? He could be a half-breed. The wolves will track us more easily if he stays.'

Nansaa sweeps up crumbs of cheese and rubs them between her fingers.

'He's only little, though.'

Buena stops work and places the uncut cheese carefully on the cloth. She turns to her daughter. 'Hold out your hand and straighten it like mine.' Nansaa looks at her in puzzlement. 'Now bite your palm,' Buena tells her.

Nansaa tries again and again. 'It won't work,' she says impatiently.

'Are you sure?' asks Buena.

Reluctant to be defeated, Nansaa tries again. She bursts out laughing. Try as she may, her teeth will not close on flesh. Nansaa's palm is like a frozen stream that refuses to quench her thirst.

'You see,' says her mother, 'you can't have everything – even when it's tantalisingly close.' She takes the cheese back out of the cloth. 'Take the dog back, Nansaa.' Buena draws the thread through the cheese.

Nansaa is mounted on the horse, ready to ride out with the sheep and goats to the grazing grounds. She has permission to stand in for her father during his absence. Her instructions are to stay near the camp and to leave Zochor at the cave.

The horse, sheep and goats know their respective roles. Accustomed to the routine, the family's oldest horse follows leisurely after the flock. The upper Bouroldjuut Valley is familiar territory.

Nansaa envisages herself as a great leader, commander of her four-legged troop. She steers the horse to the front of the flock, but as soon as she gets there, the animals turn tail and make for camp. Are the sheep going to return without her? It would be so embarrassing! Nansaa is a good little rider, as she proved last summer at the Naadam festival, celebrating Mongolia's national day. But Zochor is little help. Barking excitedly he scatters the herd in all directions instead of driving the animals behind the horse.

At last Nansaa realises that she will never succeed in rewriting the rules of herding. She slows and falls in with the unhurried pace of the meandering flock. On reaching the river valley, the animals decide that it is time to take a break. Nansaa washes her hands and tries in vain to bite her palm.

Zochor comes bounding and splashing through the water. 'Hey, Zochor, maybe you can bite it for me!' He takes a quick sniff at Nansaa's palm but loses interest as soon as he realises there is nothing to eat. 'You can't do it either, huh?' Cocking his head, the dog looks at her intently. 'Zochor, do you want to stay with me or go back to your cave?'

11

At lunchtime Buena takes the opportunity to get on with some sewing. Having collected the milk, then boiled and processed it and distilled some milk vodka, she finally has a moment to herself. Nansaa's new blue deel, the traditional robe, is nearly finished. She stiffens the collar with an iron warmed by the dung-fuelled fire.

Nansalmaa, bent over her sister's exercise book, is absorbed in sketching an imaginary city. Batbayar in the meantime has found himself a motorcycle – the sewing machine. There are no handlebars on his antiquated vehicle, let alone an exhaust, yet he accelerates all the time. Batbayar's lips form a series of impressive engine noises that grow steadily louder. Setting aside her iron, Buena applies the brakes and lifts her son from the machine. The revs give way to a plaintive whine.

Batbayar's cries make little impression on his mother. Buena feeds the collar into the machine. The stiff fabric jams beneath the foot, and Nansalmaa is called on to tug from the opposite side.

'Who is it for?'

'Your sister. For when she goes to school.'

'Will she be gone for as long as before?'

'I expect so.'

'It's no fun playing with Batbayar all the time!'

Buena turns the handle and the machine starts to whirr and judder once more.

The terrain changes under Nansaa's feet. The earth becomes stonier, the dry pats fewer and farther between.

Drinking milk tea beside the stream.

Nansaa spits on her hand and lets the little dog lick it. 'That's settled then. You and I are friends now and your new name is Zochor.'

Buena has her misgivings about the dog, but the children don't notice.

She-yaks are capable of producing up to fifteen litres per day. A family like the Batchuluuns would typically process between forty and sixty litres per day, depending on the herd's productivity.

Overleaf: Nansaa
searches for her dog.
Her calls reverberate
through the valley.

'Emee, will I be born again as a person?'
The old woman holds the needle upright and pours rice from above. Like dancing hailstones the grains come to rest in the waiting bronze dish. Grains of rice come close to the needle, almost meeting but never quite.

'You see, my child, that's how hard it is to be born again as a person.'

The Deel

Yesterday my mother was young and beautiful.
Yesterday I walked as a child beside her soft deel.
How many years has she been in this world?
How long has she been wearing her green silk deel?

MONGOLIAN FOLK SONG

53

The marketplace in Ulaanbaatar. We wander through long halls, looking at fabrics. My three female companions are excited. It's hot and we are tired from weeks of filming, but this is the only opportunity for my friends to buy material for their deels. After two months of anticipation, they can finally choose. The range of materials is limited in the countryside and my friends are anxious to make the right selection before they fly home.

Every detail must be perfect. The colour of the material, its quality, the cut, the length, the trimmings as well as the question of which style would suit whom, have all been the subject of daily debate.

Every woman we encountered during filming became a template for the planned souvenirs. Despite seeing countless photos and films, the crew did not realise until they arrived that traditional Mongolian dress is more than merely ceremonial. They were astonished when the noble-looking deel turned out to be a practical item of clothing; an everyday outfit masquerading as an ornate gown.

The male members of the crew bought their fabrics from an itinerant trader. They settled on plain materials and dull colours, convinced that brown or grey deels would be more acceptable in Europe.

Their female colleagues, still undecided about their choice of deel, watched enviously as the men were initiated. The ceremony is usually reserved for young people, but since none of those involved had ever worn a deel, we decided to count them as children. I joined the Mongolians in reciting blessings for our German friends:

The foal comes to the front.
The lambs and the kids to the back.
The things of this world are ephemeral.
May their owner be eternal.

The blessings were accompanied by a kiss and a small gift.

When I heard all the women's questions I stopped wondering why the choice of deel inspired such trepidation. How are deels made? What kind of fabrics are used? What is the significance of the trimmings and the sash? I never imagined that a single item of clothing could generate so many questions.

I explained that a deel was an uncomplicated garment to make: first the fabric is folded into three, with the length of the folded material corresponding to the length of the finished deel. Next the material is cut along a 'Z' shaped line. One of the pieces is reversed, then the two halves are sewn together. This method does away with the need for a seam between the tunic and the sleeves and allows the wearer to move freely without the fabric riding up.

Without my deel I feel naked on the steppe. For me it is a practical garment. Nomads never own more than they need, and this is exemplified by their dress. The front of the deel

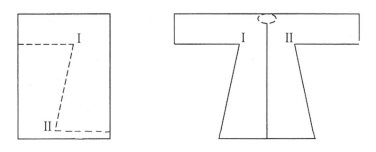

overlaps from left to right, creating a pouch at chest level. This pocket also serves as a carrying sling for babies and can always be accessed by the wearer's right hand. The deel's long sleeves also function as gloves, protecting the hands during outside chores. Women wear a narrower cut and bind their sash more tightly round their waist. The length of the robe comes in handy, ensuring a degree of privacy when nature calls on the steppe.

The drapers' stalls extend into the distance. My friends are examining some shimmering silks. They still have to decide on the design of the buttons, the colour of the trimmings and the type of lining.

The saleswomen recommend a lining made of Russian felt. The woollen material, made of coarse natural fibres in muted colours, is much more expensive than the extravagantly coloured artificial silks that my German friends are considering for the outer fabric. The choice of colours and designs available in the capital seems overwhelming after two months of living in basic conditions, miles from any kind of shop.

I act as their interpreter and negotiate on their behalf. At last my friends settle on daring combinations of artificial Chinese silk. They are proud of their choice until they hear the price – the equivalent of one euro per metre. The high cost of genuine silk would have pleased them more.

Later they are excited to discover Mongolian riding boots and cheap imitation Puma and Adidas sportswear.

Boots

When I tripped as a child
The grassland broke my fall.

MONGOLIAN POEM

The secret of a Mongolian boot lies in the toes. The upturned tip allows the foot to roll smoothly over the ground. The Mongolians show their respect for nature even in their handmade boots. The curved soles tread lightly over the grassland, sparing the stalks of the plants. At the tip of the boot, a gap between the felt or fur lining and the leather exterior insulates the foot and allows the toes to move freely.

A boot's value can be measured by the intricacy of its decorations. Embossed designs reflect the wearer's age and the occasion. A bride and groom should wear boots with thirty-six patterns. At an age ceremony, boots should feature a minimum of fifty-four designs.

Mongolian boots are made to fit either foot. Riding on horseback abrades the leather on one side, so swapping the boots between feet allows them to wear out equally on either side, ensuring that they last longer.

12

The clouds jostle for position in the sky, obstructing the sunbeams on their path to earth. Nansaa follows the flock along the side of a gorge. Boredom has set in and she is tired and hungry too. She has been riding for hours with nothing to distract her but the mind-numbingly slow grazing of sheep and goats on thyme leaves. Her eyelids are beginning to close when the horse comes to a halt. The sheep scatter in fright, clearing a path in front of her. Lying ahead is a creature the size of a billy goat. The horse jigs nervously on the spot, shifting its weight from hoof to hoof. Suddenly it backs away.

Nansaa is almost thrown from the saddle. The animal stares through her, sunlight glinting on its fangs. Nansaa's instinct is to flee. She tugs frantically at the reins but the horse ignores her and follows the startled sheep. She is right beside the lifeless body. Flies swarm over the creature's eyes and a bitter stench fills her nostrils. The wolf is dead.

As the horse breaks into a gallop, Nansaa grabs its mane. The scattered sheep have regrouped and Nansaa allows herself to be carried along behind them. She looks back helplessly as Zochor stays behind and barks.

'Here, Zochor! Hurry up!'

The mighty beast of the steppe, known to Nansaa only through its nocturnal howls, is awe-inspiring, even in death. Zochor, still barking, sidles closer to the corpse. Was Batchuluun right? Nansaa would give anything to have him here right now.

She hurries to catch up with the flock. Swinging her whip, she feels the old horse submit to her command. The scent of herbs intensifies in the humid air. The last patch of blue has vanished from the sky, sealed over by a layer of cloud. Nansaa scans her surroundings, trying to get her bearings so she can lead the flock home. Her mind is too taken up with Zochor to focus on the animals or the route.

Her dog had shown no fear at the sight of the corpse. The wolf must have been an acquaintance from Zochor's days in the cave.

Her father had been right.

The thought is somehow reassuring. Now Zochor is gone, the animals much calmer too. The dog caused nothing but trouble in the flock. Nansaa keeps the sheep moving steadily along the river bank. A black-headed lamb struggles to keep pace with its mother and begins to lag behind. The other animals graze on the hoof, but this little lamb is lazily gluttonous, stopping at each and every blade. Nansaa dismounts impatiently but the lamb refuses to be caught. Skipping neatly from side to side, it runs almost as fast as Zochor. Nansaa gathers the reins and walks beside the horse.

What if her father were wrong?

Nansaa drives the animals onwards: 'Tschaak, tschaak, tschaak!' It takes a good deal of effort to place her left foot in the stirrup. Gathering her strength, she swings herself up and grabs the mane to steady herself. Once seated, she gives a tug on the reins and turns the horse around.

Zochor is just a puppy. He must have known the wolf was dangerous and wanted to protect her.

Zochor is alone.

Nansaa slides down from the saddle. Taking care to keep her footing on the rocky terrain, she edges closer to the precipice.

A gorge extends beneath her, the Suman river winding its way along the bottom. Last winter a man and his flock were pulled over the edge during a violent storm.

'Zochor! Zochor!' Nansaa shouts for her dog. 'Zochor! Zochor!' The only sound is her echo.

13

Thunder rumbles in the distance. A dazzling flash of lightning announces the onset of the storm. Buena runs to fetch more water before the rain can muddy the stream. Her eyes sweep the steppe. The grassy banks have the rich green vibrancy that she longs to see each summer, but away from the water's edge the pastures are bleached. The grasses and herbs will be grateful for the downpour.

Glancing up, she catches sight of the flock on the ridge. It is good to know that Nansaa has taken a short cut and will make it home in time. The animals trot briskly down the escarpment. Buena hastily brings the store of dried dung inside the shelter of the ger. She is just snatching up the washing from the sheep pen when the flock appears in the valley.

Nansaa is not there.

Buena thinks quickly. Is the flock complete? Her daughter could be rounding up stragglers on the far side of the hill. She does a quick headcount. No animals are missing.

Nansaa is not there.

Batbayar and Nansalmaa are waiting inside the ger for their meal of fresh yoghurt. Buena prepares their lunch with prac-tised movements but her real concern is for Nansaa.

'I'm going to look for your sister,' Buena tells the younger children. Batbayar enjoys his lunch without a care. He likes this time of day. As far as he is concerned, things could hardly be better. Slurping his yoghurt, he smacks his lips. He wants to prove that he can eat on his own.

'Nansalmaa, you'll have to look after your brother for me.' Buena runs a cloth over Batbayar's yoghurt mous-tache. She steps into the open air. Once outside, she loosens the straps around the roof and closes the roof ring in case it starts to rain. While she is fetching her horse, she hears Nansalmaa raise her voice in song. Her daughter chants loudly and clearly, barely stopping to breathe. The little girl knows exactly what is expected of her: Batbayar must not be allowed to notice that his mother is riding away.

Food

Stalks of grain sway gently in the breeze.
Birds of passage screech above.
The airak tastes stronger –
Such is the colour of autumn.

MONGOLIAN FOLK SONG

It is 11 July, at the height of the German summer a few years ago. The plan is to spend Naadam, our national day, with some fellow Mongolians from Munich. We decide to celebrate in the countryside. We will have to make do without wrestling, archery or horse racing, but khorkhog will be served. Khorkhog, which roughly translates as 'mutton in a sealed milk pan', is seen by non-Mongolians as our national dish.

The recipe is very simple – rather like preparing lasagne. A layer of warm stones is placed in a milk pan and covered with chunks of meat on the bone. Another layer of warm stones follows, then seasoned mutton or fresh vegetables, if any are available. The dish is topped by a final layer of stones. Water is added and the pan sealed tightly.

We head for the fields to hunt for stones. They bear little resemblance to the nuggets of rounded rock that we find in Mongolian rivers. These stones are angular and frustratingly elusive. Our collection is meagre but we heat the stones anyway and put the ingredients in the pan. We place our Mongolian pressure cooker over the flames, turning it while we wait.

The meal is a disaster. The German stones shatter under the temperature and pressure, splinters grinding between our teeth.

At home I clasp a warm stone in my hands before eating. Its surface feels soothing. Stress and other negative emotions are absorbed by the rock.

*

'Mutton in a milk pan': this description points to the key elements of the Mongolian diet – meat and milk.

With its short hot summers and long cold winters, Central Asia has a climate ranging from plus forty to minus forty degrees, making it ill-suited to arable farming. Only the hardiest vegetables – sugar beet, carrots, cabbage and potatoes – survive.

Like their ancestors, the nomads rely on animal products for sustenance. The Mongolians' favourite meat is mutton. Nothing is left except the glands. My father saw the sheep's head as a particular delicacy and always let me eat the tongue. According to him it was especially good for craftsmanship and creativity.

Goats are seldom used for meat as their principal value is in producing cashmere for luxury goods. In the Gobi Desert and other arid regions there are no yaks and few cows, so goats and sheep are milked instead.

Camel meat forms part of the nomads' diet, although traditional camel farming is in decline. These days cars are usurping the camel's time-honoured role as a beast of burden. Besides, a female camel foals just once in two years and the camel's warm but coarse wool is less valuable than goat's hair. Nowadays camels are kept primarily for their meat, which the nomads sell or barter. Camel flesh can be grilled, boiled or smoked. The motivation for smoking meat has nothing to do with taste, unlike in the West. Smoking is the nomads' only available means of food preservation and is used to dry the meat and seal it from flies' eggs.

Mongolians smoke their meat over a fire fuelled by dung. Their preferred fuel is blue dung – blueish pats of she-yak dung, dried over the course of several years. The drier the pats, the less intrusive the taste of dung.

Needless to say, Mongolians can no more survive on a permanent diet of meat than anyone else. In summertime the nomads avoid meat altogether. The pastures are fresher and there is more grassland for grazing, so the milk yield increases and dairy products are eaten instead. These are processed daily.

The quantity of milk produced varies with the seasons and with the animals' age. She-yaks are capable of producing up to fifteen litres per day. A family such as Batchuluun's would process between forty and sixty litres per day, depending on the productivity of the herd. Usually it is the task of one woman to milk the cows twice daily and churn the milk in the banag, the separate, smaller ger used for kitchen tasks. Yak milk contains roughly 7 per cent fat and is converted into curd cheese, yoghurt, cheese, butter and cream.

The nomads boil their green tea in milk and season it with salt. My German friends compared the brew to a soup or broth. At certain times of the year it is served with roasted rice. The tea is salted for good reason. In Mongolia's extremely arid continental climate it is important for the body to retain its precious minerals.

Airak, fermented mare's milk, is another popular dairy product. It is served to visitors from July until late autumn. The alcohol content is initially low and the beverage has a mild laxative effect. As the summer progresses, the alcohol content rises and by autumn, the season of festivities, the milk is comparable to 'yellow airak', the Mongolian term for foreign beer.

Numerous berries – blueberries, cranberries, strawberries and sea buckthorn berries – grow wild in Mongolia as do various cereals. Knotgrass is incredibly scarce and has the status of a delicacy on the barren steppe.

The field mice are expert at collecting knotgrass, thereby saving their human neighbours the effort. The nomads raid the rodents' stores but never help themselves to more than half the share. Knotgrass seeds are used to prepare treats that are usually saved for special guests. The seed is mixed with warm cream and served as a sweet or savoury delicacy. It is said that a child who tastes a morsel the size of a fingernail holds a star within his reach. When I came across marzipan in a German supermarket I remembered our knotgrass concoctions and my mouth began to water.

When I was young I never saw the sense of leaving half the rare and precious grain in the mouse's stash. Why not take more? My uncle gave me a solemn look. A person's greed could drive a mouse to suicide, he told me. Mice had been known to hang themselves on blades of grass. He described the process so vividly and exactly that I have yet to find anyone who can disprove it.

14

'Zochor! Zochor!'

When Batchuluun loses an animal, he stations himself on a hilltop and looks for movement in the valley. He often forgets his binoculars and Nansaa must fetch them for him. Now she stands alone on the hill, with only her eyes to rely on.

She scans the valley in vain. The sky and steppe stretch into the distance. Swollen clouds glare at her, almost grazing her head. She feels a few raindrops, falling hesitantly at first. An angry, dark mass sweeps over the horizon. From her vantage point she spots a winter camp at the far end of the valley. Nansaa points her horse towards it. Child and cloud pit themselves against each other on the godforsaken steppe.

Over the summer, the nomads prefer to camp in the open valley, but in winter they take refuge at the foot of the mountain, sheltered from the wind and snow. The camp has been abandoned for some time. Still, Nansaa will wait there until the storm has passed.

A flash of lightning arcs across the sky. They are halfway to camp when the downpour begins. Nansaa spurs on from a trot to a gallop. Her horse, more focused with every stride, has guessed where they are heading. It battles against the wind that buffets them, pelting Nansaa's face with rain. The young girl's heels dig into the stirrups as she crouches over the mane. The cloud is already upon them. As the horse's hooves strike the ground, they send up a cloud of earth behind them.

At last horse and rider slow to a trot. Just a few more paces and the horse can stop entirely. It breathes heavily, nostrils quivering. Nansaa slides weakly from the saddle.

The wooden stalls are eerily quiet. Nansaa has chosen a deserted place in which to shelter from the fury of the storm. The rain is heavier than ever.

Senses alert, she slips cautiously into a stall. A beam has worked its way loose from the ceiling and hangs loose above her. The ground is soft and warm and the air smells of dung. The occasional tuft of grass protrudes from the soil. Nansaa spots an ox-cart with its wheels removed.

In wintertime her family shares a camp with her father's brothers and their animals. This camp is big enough to accommodate seven or eight families at least. Outside the rain seems heavier than ever, stamping on the roof like thousands of miniature feet. Angry raindrops roar in her ears. She peers outside and is comforted to see that her old horse seems a little rested already and is grazing placidly in the storm. She gazes at it as it chews and then notices a dead marmot lying nearby.

She catches her breath.

'Zochor!'

On their way home from the cave Zochor had caught and killed a marmot. She had kept the story to herself in case it reflected badly on him.

Nansaa rushes into the next stall, calling for her dog.

'Zochor! Zochor!'

The stall is empty.

She runs to the next. Her dog is crouched in the corner of a nursing pen. He is dry and seems well-fed. She takes him by the paw.

15

'Don't lose sight of the big mountain,' Buena had instructed Nansaa that morning when she was leaving with the flock. Now the summits are covered in cloud. The rain has stopped, so Nansaa sets off in what she hopes is the right direction. Zochor comes too.

Her path since that morning has been set by the flock. The animals are probably home by now. Nansaa wishes the sheep were there to guide her. She listens intently. There is singing in the distance. She follows the lingering melody through the dusk.

A ger, draped in blue, comes as a welcome sight. She no longer feels quite so alone in this unfamiliar place. The dwelling is smaller than usual, with no more than seven or eight goats tethered outside. Nansaa strains her ears but the voice has fallen silent. A tiny female figure hobbles from the tent. The woman's white hair is clipped close to her head and she smiles an impish smile.

Once the horse is tied to the pen, the old woman helps Nansaa from the saddle. Zochor is in the ger already. The woman says little, ushering Nansaa towards the warmth as though the visit had been planned. Nansaa is too tired to wonder why she forgoes the usual welcome ceremony. Her mind feels empty. She willingly submits to the stranger, who removes her sodden deel and dries her wet hair. A bowl of tea warms her hands.

The ger is filled with flickering light from the stove. A sour smell has taken up residence in the dark goat furs on the floor and the embroidered mandalas on the walls. Strips of dried meat hang from the struts overhead.

The old woman gives Zochor a metal cup to drink from. 'It's a good job your dog didn't fall into the cave of the yellow dog,' she says slowly, stroking Zochor. Nansaa is emboldened by the warmth of the tea inside her and the familiarity of the woman's gestures.

'Emee, why is it called the cave of the yellow dog?' she plucks up the courage to ask.

'A poor dog had a terrible time there,' says the old woman and tells Nansaa the story of the dreaded cave.

'A long time ago there was a rich couple with a beautiful daughter and a yellow dog. The daughter was their only child and one day she fell ill. Medicine couldn't cure her so the father asked a wise man for advice. The old sage told him: 'You need to send your yellow dog away.'

On hearing this advice the father asked, 'But why? Is there something wrong with him?'

The sage replied: 'You requested my advice and I gave it. Now the decision rests with you.'

Even though the dog had served the family faithfully for years, the man was prepared to do anything for his daughter's sake. He decided to give the dog away. But everyone had heard that the dog was angry, so no one was willing to take it. The idea of killing the yellow dog was too much for the man. He hid it in a cave and brought food to it every day.

Sure enough, his daughter got well. The truth was, she had fallen in love with an impoverished carver. The yellow dog had guarded her so closely that the young man couldn't visit. The girl had been lovesick. Without the dog to stop their meetings, she soon got well.'

Zochor has been lazing by the shrine. He gets to his feet and gives himself a shake. The woman is holding a set of prayer beads. She has been slipping the dried berries deftly through her fingers throughout her story. She smiles at Nansaa.

'But tell me, Emee, what happened to the yellow dog?'

'One day the father took food to the cave as usual, but the yellow dog had vanished. The daughter married the carver and in time she gave birth to a child. Maybe the dog was reborn with a ponytail.'

The rain has stopped.

The Cave of the Yellow Dog

Whether I will be or not be
My voice will be sung by the songbirds
Proud as ever the sky above
Many people will remain.

MONGOLIAN FOLK SONG

As a young girl I often felt neglected. I had a tendency to fall ill, so my parents would leave me behind when they went on long trips. I spent the summer holidays at my grandmother's while the rest of my family, including my younger siblings, joined my uncle at our winter camp in Khorgo. They were gone for weeks or months on end.

Afterwards they would tell stories about a place that haunted my imagination for years: the Cave of the Yellow Dog.

The picture I had formed was of a deep cavern, dark and forbidding, sunken into a rock-strewn lava landscape – a place of stories and secrets. The floor was littered with innumerable white bones and animal skeletons. Hungry wolves dragged their prey there to devour it undisturbed.

Many years later, in the spring of 2004, I paid my first visit to the cave. Together with a group of Korean tourists I peered inside and was confronted with the geological facts: situated at an altitude of 2260 metres above sea level, the cave forms a forty-metre wide and ten-metre deep recess in the rock. The stone chamber echoes with birdsong and the beating of wings.

I noted with surprise that the grey lava floor was covered in grasses and berry plants. The neighbouring volcano is thought to have been extinct for the past ten to twenty thousand years. The action of wind and vapour on the molten lava led to the creation of ten or so caves of varying sizes, among them the Cave of the Yellow Dog or 'Hell of the Yellow

The eldest child, Nansaa, is the image of her father.

According to official
statistics, 41 per cent
of Mongolians live on
the land. Increasingly,
nomads are
considering migrating
to the city.

Batchuluun returns
from the city with gifts
for all the family.

Nomadic families see their stoves as sacred. During a wedding ceremony the bride consents to marriage by lighting a fire, thus calling a new family into being.

'*Om mani padme hum.*' According to Buddhist teaching, life is like a swamp. When Buddha attained enlightenment he rose through the mire and blossomed like a lotus flower. Man is the only living being capable of transcending earthly suffering.

Look at your father's present! Accustomed to her metal ladle, Buena had forgotten to remove her new gift from the stove.

Dog', as it is known. Since 'hell' has a wholly negative meaning in the West, we modified the translation to account for the divergence in cultural meaning.

Scattered around this place of legend are stones bearing the imprint of sea creatures and marine vegetation, a clear indication that the area, now so far from the sea, was once submerged in water. According to the nomads, the fossilised creatures are ancient birds. The sea for most Mongolians is an alien concept.

The film project and my encounter with the old woman, whose rendering of the legend was so vivid and compelling, rekindled my childhood memory, restoring to the cave some of its original allure. I saw bones at the base of the dark cavern and imagined the skeleton of the yellow dog. I saw wooden stakes on the floor and imagined the animal's owner climbing down a ladder with tidbits of food. I stared into the depths and pictured my mother as a child, gazing down, searching like me for proof of the legend.

I stood above the cave, birds soaring beneath my feet.

16

Buena lights a candle. She has just returned with Nansaa. The young girl and the puppy were sheltering with an old woman and her eight goats, only a few valleys away from the family's camp. Nansaa should have known her way back – they had lived in that area before she went away to school – but the rain and mist had disoriented her. No doubt Batchuluun will be displeased to see the puppy, but Buena has no objection to her daughter's new companion.

Batbayar and Nansalmaa are asleep on the floor, surrounded by pastry crumbs and shreds of dried cheese. The statue of Buddha has been moved from its home on the altar and is tucked up in bed.

'My two little elves!' Buena undresses her children gently, glad to have everyone under one roof.

Nansaa slips beneath the covers. 'Mother, can you remember what it was like in your past lives?' She speaks in a whisper so as not to wake her siblings.

'I don't think so.'

'Why not?'

'Maybe only children can remember. When children make up stories, they're remembering their past lives, or so people say.'

'Did I make up stories?'

'All kinds of them.' Buena smiles to herself.

'Tell me one!'

'Shush, be quiet now. It's time to sleep.'

Nansaa tries to remember the stories she used to tell. Before Buena can tuck her sister in beside her, she is fast asleep and dreaming of the little blue ger.

'Emee, will I be born again as a person?'

The old woman laughs knowingly, her crooked fingers turning the prayer wheel. Another peal of silvery laughter rises from her fragile body. Her tongue, deserted by her teeth, moves alone in her empty mouth.

'Look, little one, I've got something to show you.'

She takes a handful of rice and a needle. The old woman holds the silvery point upright, showering rice from above. Like dancing hailstones the grains come to rest in the waiting bronze dish. Grains of rice and the tip of a needle, almost meeting but never quite. The old woman pours more rice, keeps pouring.

'Be sure to tell me if a grain lands on the needle.'

She keeps pouring, over and over again. Grains of rice bounce into the dish and the tip of the needle is unchanged. The rice streams past.

The old woman laughs a warm laugh. 'You see, my child, that's how hard it is to be born again as a person.'

Rice falls from her tiny hands. Born a person, born a dog, born a person, born an animal. She keeps pouring.

Music

The dainty foal is peaceful
Stroke its hoof as you saddle it.
Things are not easy in strange territory.
Patiently adapt.

The dainty foal is gentle
Pull the reins softly whilst mounting
Things are not easy in strange territory
Adapt to your surroundings with love.

MONGOLIAN FOLK SONG

There are many ways in which I have adjusted to life in Germany and there is plenty about the culture that I like. But one side of life continues to defeat me – parties. I find the noise and the cigarette smoke unbearable.

When I first arrived in Germany I often heard the same advice: never miss a party if you want to make contacts. I was baffled. Was I supposed to elbow my way through crowded rooms, shouting at people's backs and introducing myself at top volume?

As far as I'm concerned, celebrating with friends means singing. A party, by definition, entails singing and fresh air. For Mongolians, including my generation of city-dwellers, a good party or even a long car journey must always involve a singing contest.

My favourite lama features in one of my films. He can sing all night without repeating a single song, which is one of the reasons I admire him. Even in Ulaanbaatar people get together in their modern apartments and hold singing competitions with their neighbours. People seldom complain. We sing of love, nature, our mothers, fathers and, above all, our horses. Our songs are where we hide our sorrow and our joy.

Legend has it that the sound of the horse-head violin can comfort mourning souls. The story of the two-stringed fiddle tells of a man who lost his favourite horse. After the horse's death, the man grieved day and night. The horse would talk to him in his sleep, appearing before him as clear as day. Eager to have his beloved friend's company in his waking hours as well, the man cut off the dead horse's head and placed it on the neck of a violin. He made strings from the tendons and took hairs from its tail for the bow. Its skin was stretched over the instrument's body. Now the horse could speak to him whenever he called, replying in melancholy song. The man took comfort in his horse-head violin. Playing the instrument was like galloping on his horse.

Overtone singing or khuumii singing was born of a similar need. According to one of many legends, this renowned vocal style was developed in order to soothe a weeping mother camel whose colt had been lost in a raging river. Her cries of grief were so piteous that the camel's owner mimicked the lost colt's calls with his voice.

An overtone singer can elicit two tones simultaneously. The singer's trained diaphragm works in conjunction with the muscles of the gut to maintain the base tone, over which the melody is sung. Vocalising the melody requires great physical effort from the throat, tongue, windpipe and mouth. Children learning the technique often suffer from sore throats after singing for any length of time. A khuumii singer's body is like a wind instrument.

The urtiin duu or 'long song' requires similar technical mastery. Although the breathing is free, the singer must adhere to strict rules of performance and pause as infrequently as possible, never breathing during a melodic ornament. Long songs have continuously flowing melodies, wide pitch intervals and rhythmical variation. They are sung in verses without refrains, using the full register of the singer's voice. Nomads traditionally sing long songs during slow solitary journeys on horseback on the steppe. The songs express the vastness and freedom of the Mongolian landscape. They are used to mark calendar celebrations and day-to-day rites.

The bogino duu or 'short song' is performed without melodic ornaments. This singing style adheres to a fixed rhythm. Short songs can be improvised, giving the singer an opportunity to satirise friends or particular incidents.

Magtaal or 'praise songs' are performed in honour of the spirits of nature. They are sung to pay homage to the mountains, rivers or nature in general. Magtaal have been sung for centuries and the tradition is kept alive by the people of the Mongolian Altai, the mountain range in the west of Mongolia. Praise songs are more rhythmical than long songs and contain more lyrics.

As a child, I was especially interested in tuuli. Like classical myths, these epic songs commemorate the deeds of past heroes. The songs use a highly poetic form to describe the fierce battle between the powers of good and evil.

Traditionally, tuuli accompanied certain fixed rituals and were thought to have a magical effect. Nomads believed the melodies would exorcise evil spirits and curry favour with the forces of nature. They were usually performed at the start of a hunt or a battle, to ward off illness or infertility, or to while away the winter nights.

Mongolian games, music and dances vary with the seasons. Inside the ger, dances are performed with less expansive movements, sheep's anklebones are used to play dice, and fables are told or sung to lend cheer to the long cold evenings.

Epic songs can be performed over a number of weeks but my grandmother's tuuli continued indefinitely. I often had the impression that she added stories invented purely for our benefit. The songs really only ended with her death. Now tuuli are a tourist attraction and are performed in shortened form.

Pain, loss, fortune, the history of our people and the nature of our surroundings – our songs are a way of dealing with our experiences. Mongolians sing whenever there is cause for joy. But singing has also provided an outlet for our troubles. I am struck by the increasing numbers of people seeking counselling in Ulaanbaatar. The incidence of depression has risen sharply over the past few years. Maybe we need to sing more.

I miss singing. Mongolians are not interested in whether or not you can sing – everyone is expected to rise to the challenge. To us, the idea of being too ashamed to sing is incomprehensible. No matter how many arguments, objections or excuses you put forward, in Mongolia there is no such thing as not being able to sing.

My film crew was asked to sing while we were working in the Gobi Desert. After lengthy deliberation they settled on 'My hat, it has three corners', recited with the gestures. The genre excited intense debate among the nomads, who could not decide whether it was poetry or song.

17

Nansaa and her little sister Nansalmaa have retreated with Zochor to their hideout behind the gooseberry bushes. They lie back in the grass and look up at the sky.

'I see a fox.'

'I see an old man.'

The two girls are finding treasure in the clouds. When one of them spots a figure in the sky, she must convince the other of its existence. If both agree, the animal or shape belongs to whoever found it first. They are already fantastically wealthy.

Today they must work with particular speed. At any moment their assets could be blown away by the wind.

Nansalmaa fights to protect her fortune. She finds the most amazing creatures in the sky.

'The giraffe is mine!' She desperately wants to win.

'That's not a giraffe.'

'It is too!'

Nansaa sits up. 'How do you know? You've never seen one!'

'I don't care. I know it's a giraffe. And it's mine!'

Nansaa nobly concedes defeat.

Buena is crouched behind a plume of smoke. 'Stay away from the smoke,' she tells Batbayar, who is tossing dung in the air. She steers him to one side. Buena has strung a leg of mutton from the shaft of an ox-cart. She lights the blue dung, dried by the action of wind and sun, and smokes the meat above it.

Nansaa comes running with Zochor, bursting to tell her something.

'Mother, Mother, Nansalmaa's been telling stories!'

Nansaa is full of excitement.

'What kind of stories?'

'Ones that aren't true! She's been talking about giraffes!'

Buena lays a restraining hand on Batbayar, who has switched to aiming stones at the mutton.

98

'Well, what do you think? Is it a story from her previous life?' Nansaa asks impatiently.

Buena attends to her grumpy son whose nostrils are full of acrid smoke.

'Perhaps … But let Nansalmaa tell stories if she wants.'

18

Nansaa jumps up. 'Quick, Zochor, over here!' Zochor is busy chasing a grasshopper, oblivious to the urgency. The motor-cycle closes steadily on the camp. Nansaa chases after her dog, grabs him by the scruff of the neck and drags him behind the banag.

Batchuluun pulls up next to the ox-cart. He dusts off his hat. Nansaa is doing everything in her power to hush the struggling Zochor. It would all be over if he barked!

Her father enters the ger. 'How was the trip?' asks Buena. She hands her husband some tea, then clears the table hurriedly so she can set out the welcome fare and continue with her work. Using a bodkin, she threads a ribbon through some strips of cheese. Later she will suspend them from the spokes overhead.

'Everything went to plan. I sold the skins.'

'How is brother Dorj and his family?'

'They're well. We spoke about Nansaa. She can stay with them when she goes back to school.'

'Is business good?'

Batchuluun recounts how his brother had barely a moment to spare. With such a queue of people to see him, he was far too busy for a quiet bowl of tea. He was obviously doing well, though. Many of the other ex-nomads were struggling to survive. 'Down-at-heel, unemployed, addicted to archi – and they come to Dorj for help.'

It is time for some gifts. Batchuluun hands Buena a new ladle: 'There, didn't I promise you?'

'Look how light and pretty it is! Green like the grass – and so bright it almost glows!'

Gratified by the success of his gift, Batchuluun produces a second package wrapped in newspaper.

'A torch, how useful,' says Buena. She picks up the old newspaper and studies the headlines.

'How did the elections go?' she asks.

Mongolia's fourth general election took place this

summer. Neither the communists nor the democrats were happy with the outcome, necessitating a return to the polls. This year Batchuluun and Buena are making more of an effort to keep abreast of the political situation. The time has come to think seriously about moving to the city.

'The new campaigns were very expensive, I hear.'

Nansaa has been struggling with Zochor behind the banag. Her parents' conversation has mostly passed her by. Now, she is filled with the urge to see her presents right away. She needs to find a way of stopping Zochor from bounding up to Batchuluun. She jams the dung basket over his head. 'I'll be right back,' she promises.

By the time she reaches the ger, Nansalmaa and Batbayar are right behind her. They storm inside together, galvanised by the prospect of sugary treats. In no time their expectations are rewarded and they each clutch a sweet. The special occasion comes with a reminder from Buena: 'Take care of your teeth!' Nansalmaa folds the shiny wrapping carefully and licks delicately at the sweet. Batbayar pops his inside his mouth, wrapping and all. Nansaa tries to fish out the package before he swallows it whole.

Amid the hubbub of greetings and presents, Batchuluun brings out another gift. He deposits a pink furry creature on the low table. Batbayar makes a grab for it but his father holds him back.

'Wait, I'll show you how it works.'

Spellbound, the three children stare at the odd-looking thing.

With a flick of a switch, the ball of fur comes to life. Its bright green eyes flash maniacally and it emits a piercing squeal. It can even wag its tail! The toy is a tiny dog that walks of its own accord.

The children swoop on their new plaything, each eager to touch it. Batbayar gets a hold of its fluffy fur and the dog is lifted, legs flailing, into the air. They all laugh.

Zochor barks.

He has escaped from the dung basket, slunk under the raised felt awning and is squeezing his way through the ger's latticed wall. With a growl he pounces on the toy. Before he has a chance to bite, Batchuluun bats him away.

'Nansaa,' he says in a stern voice, 'why is the dog still here?'

She maintains a defiant silence.

'The dog stays behind when we leave.'

Nansaa's baby brother takes advantage of the sudden reversal of mood to claim the little pink dog for himself.

Political Change

It is better to be the head of a fly
than the tail of a tiger.

MONGOLIAN PROVERB

I was seventeen years old and still at school in 1989 when the
political upheaval began. At the start of the year, 57 per cent
of the two-million-strong population lived in Ulaanbaatar

and other urban centres, while 43 per cent of all Mongolians lived on the land. The collapse of communism had far-reaching consequences, both for pastoral nomads and city-dwellers like me. At first we had to pluck up the courage to discuss the anti-government pamphlets during break-times. We spoke in a whisper for fear of arrest.

In the late 1930s thousands of anti-government intellectuals and lamas had been killed by the regime. Even on the eve of revolution, critics of the government ran the risk of imprisonment.

Decree No. 20 was passed in January 1991 and caused 100 per cent inflation overnight, revealing the true state of our country to many of my compatriots. The papers carried pictures of shop-assistants dressed in white tabards, waiting helplessly in empty stores. The shelves offered nothing but salt. We ate roasted rice tea morning, midday and night.

Our vocabulary grew to include a host of new words – perestroika, rally, hunger strike, provisional government, democracy. Blue flags fluttered in the street and loudspeakers denounced the 'Russian lapdogs' in power. We broadcast our rage throughout the land. The people were right.

In the next street, marchers waved red flags and chanted slogans about free education and healthcare. Not long afterwards my dream of going to drama school became too expensive to contemplate. These people were right as well. Who was telling the truth? I spent the next few years in turmoil, searching for answers.

Like many of his generation, my father was a communist by conviction. We continued to argue about politics even when international aid organisations stepped in to provide our food. The city was divided. When the first multi-party elections were held in 1992, the Communists received 92 per cent of the vote. In 1996 nearly 65 per cent of Mongolians voted democrat.

The political revolution brought a gradual shift from state-owned to private property. Before long, my parents owned their apartment outright. There were rich people and poor people in the city and the steppe. In the old system, nomads with large flocks were rewarded with medals by the communists; now the animals were theirs to keep. Meanwhile, those who had fulfilled their obligations by tending smaller flocks were plunged into an economic crisis for which they were unprepared. Like many teachers, party officials and doctors, they entered the free market economy empty-handed.

Initially, there was a rise in the number of herdsmen, as many were tempted by the prospect of earning a living with animals of their own. However the price of animal and dairy products was deregulated and the state no longer provided a safety net for the herdsmen.

Until 1989 the Communist regime used the nomads as a means of feeding the nation at low cost. The government had a vested interest in keeping the nomads on the steppe. Pastoral nomads were not free to choose where they lived and could not simply migrate to the city. Young people from nomadic families could study in Ulaanbaatar but needed special permission to continue to live there. Rural girls had a reputation for being particularly sociable at university: marriage was the simplest and most reliable route to staying in the city.

Under Communist rule, nomadic families were granted private ownership of a maximum of thirty smaller animals such as sheep or goats, or ten larger animals such as horses, camels or yaks. Milk, meat, cashmere and other products were the property of the negdel, a co-operative of herders, similar to the Soviet kolkhoz. The state provided social and economic support in return.

City-dwellers such as ourselves were expected to pay a contribution towards the nomads' upkeep. Every February during my childhood we helped with the preparations for the lambing season. Schools asked for donations of candles, matches, warm blankets and gloves. My mother made padded pouches for the newborn animals from old coats.

The city had its own pastures and kept vast containers of feed. During particularly harsh winters the government would come to the aid of the herders and keep the loss of livestock to a minimum. Nowadays nomads can choose between the city and the steppe but the safety nets are gone. Herders must pay grazing fees and the increasingly arid climate has added to their woes.

Perhaps the old regime could have halted the influx to the city that started during an exceptionally cold winter ten years after democratisation. In Mongolia's third general election, over 94 per cent of the population voted for the Communists, an expression of despair and nostalgia.

Prior to 2003 the government attempted to discourage migration by taxing new arrivals. According to official statistics, 41 per cent of Mongolians still live on the land. Since many migrants avoided the taxes by failing to register, the true figure is probably closer to 25 per cent.

While I was making my graduation film last summer, I experienced the political deadlock first hand: 45 per cent of the population voted for the Democrats, 48 per cent for the Communists. In some constituencies the only solution was to return to the polls.

19

A rope leads from Zochor to one of the straps around the ger.
He whimpers. Batchuluun and Sharaw crouch beside him,
talking. The old hunter has come to collect the ammunition
that Batchuluun fetched from the city. He raises the dog's
ears and splays its paws.

'Perfect colouring for a hunting dog.'

Prising open Zochor's jaws, he inspects his teeth to check
his age. His own dog is nearing the end of its hunting days.

Sharaw is definitely interested in the puppy. Batchuluun has generously offered to make a present of it, but he refuses to be rushed.

'Was he bred from a hunting dog? Where did you get him?'

'He came home with my daughter …' Batchuluun mumbles.

Nansaa, eavesdropping on the conversation through the felt walls of the ger, knows what her father is proposing. She sees a way of turning Zochor's story to her advantage.

'He was in a cave!' she pipes up, appearing suddenly before them.

'In a cave?'

Rising to his feet, the hunter glances sceptically at Zochor and shoulders his gun.

Batchuluun loosens the rope, then ties another knot. He keeps hold of the leash, trying to buy himself a little time. When he speaks he sounds helpless and flustered: 'Nansaa, we don't even know if we'll be staying on the steppe. What if we move to the city?'

Nansaa flops next to the whimpering and cowering Zochor. She strokes her dog mournfully, knowing full well that the struggle is far from over.

Batchuluun accompanies Sharaw to his horse. He holds the gun while the hunter gets into the saddle. There is no need for explanations. The hunter's silence is enough.

20

The chores fly by with the help of the new ladle. Buena has moved on to the calves' enclosure and is straining milk through a sieve, ridding it of grass, flies and animal hairs.

Batchuluun is chopping wood. Earlier, while milking, Buena had watched him split the logs in four. He worked unusually quickly, as though he needed to chop enough wood to last them all winter.

Buena would like to tell him not to wear himself out. They

are breaking camp tomorrow and he is wasting his energy. Batchuluun is now splitting the quartered logs into even smaller sticks and Buena senses that he is in no mood for her advice. She carries the heavy pails of milk into the ger. Time is running out if she is to prepare the milk and start packing up their things before bedtime. The stove is still warm. She prods the greying embers with a poker and blows to stir them. Outside, the axe thuds dully as Batchuluun takes out his frustration on the ever-diminishing wood. Batbayar and Nansalmaa squabble over the new pink dog. Nansaa is sulking next to Zochor.

Tomorrow will be a tiring day for all the family. Buena fills her husband's silver bowl with tsiidem, milk diluted with water, and carries it out to him.

'We'll tether the dog and leave it here,' he tells her, still determinedly chopping wood. 'I'll untie it when I come back on my own for the sheep pen.'

'I'll explain to Nansaa that Zochor won't starve,' says Buena. She unbuttons the flap of her deel and fills the pouch with wood chips. She will wait until Batchuluun has finished his bowl before going inside.

'Mother, Mother, come quickly!' The children are shrieking in the ger. Buena lets the wood fall from her pouch and rushes in. There is an acrid smell in the air. A plume of black smoke rises from the stove.

'Keep back!'

Buena lifts the heavy bucket into the air and splashes water into the pan. It hisses, filling the tent with steam.

'Can I see?' Nansalmaa leans inquisitively over the stove.

'Look at your father's present!' Buena holds the bright green ladle by her fingertips, lifting it up for them to see. 'What a pity!' The plastic has melted. Accustomed to her metal ladle, she had forgotten to remove it from the stove.

Later that evening Batchuluun repairs the old ladle. The metallic thump of the hammer shatters the silence, sending scavengers screeching into the air. One by one the vultures recover from the shock and settle back down. The family's last day at the campsite is coming to a close.

'Can I play with the torch?' asks Nansalmaa.

Buena dismantles the altar, swaddling the fragile orna- ments in clothes. She is absorbed in her preparations for the move. Nansalmaa stumbles over the threshold into the dark. The torch paints pictures on the white roof of the ger. The beam roams over the surface, criss-crossing the felt. It settles on Nansaa who has retreated with Zochor behind the tent. She scowls at her younger sister.

'You can't have everything – even if it's tantalising close.'

The latticed walls are designed to maximise living space and to protect against the tearing wind. Willow or other flexible wood is used. It takes less than an hour to erect or dismantle a ger.

'We thank you, beautiful land of Khangai, for permitting us to spend our summer here.' Buena tosses spoonfuls of milk over the horses' stirrups and the wheels of each cart.

The vultures queue up
in hierarchical order,
feeding on the sheep.
Batbayar totters
towards them. The
grey birds, taller than
the child, hack at the
bones with their long
curved beaks.

Lisa Reisch and Byambasuren Davaa.

The Ger

Night-time
Is light ashamed of love.

MONGOLIAN POEM

I finally get my own two-bedroom apartment in Munich after four years in student accommodation. All that's missing is the furniture.

Despite being raised in the Mongolian capital, I am well acquainted with the simple lifestyle of the ger. Both my parents migrated to Ulaanbaatar when they were young, but in the long school holidays I stayed with my grandmother on the land. A census conducted in 2000 put the ger-dwelling urban and rural population at 61 per cent. Living in cramped conditions is a way of seeking intimacy in the vastness of a country where each inhabitant can claim a full square kilometre to himself.

In Germany, where the population is much denser, all this space belongs to me alone.

Young nomads must wait until marriage to receive a ger of their own. The tent is made especially for the newly-weds. Bride and groom are each expected to provide a bed and a wooden chest, the basis of every household. One chest is used for clothes while the other contains the family's most cherished possessions and mementos. As children, we watched my grandmother for hours, waiting until we could pinch a sweet from the chest without her seeing. The sumptuous raisins were already old and wizened and tasted of suds. They had been hidden for years with my grandmother's best soap.

Shrines are erected on top of the chest. Sticks of incense, dishes for offerings and pictures or figurines of the family's personal gods are placed there.

The left side of the ger is reserved for women, the household and the family. The right side belongs to the men and is used to store tools, saddles and guns. The middle of the ger serves as living space, while the area near the door is used for doing chores and for sheltering newborn animals when the weather is too cold.

Children under the age of fourteen are not permitted to enter the rear section of the ger when guests are being received. This area, where the place of honour is located, is the preserve of the family head and his guests.

I scan my apartment, looking for a place of honour. How about the sofa, with its view of the apartment block opposite, or the armchair in front of the TV? I begin to see why life in a ger is governed by rules, rules so numerous that I find myself explaining them to the film crew on an almost daily basis.

Some of these rules were taught to me by Nansaa. Whistling, for instance, is forbidden in a ger: the noise could entice snakes. Stepping on the threshold will bring bad luck. No one should enter a ger if a rope bars the door. The last resting place of the dead must be respected. The rope also signals the danger of disease.

Sharing a living space of twenty-four square metres with seven people demands enormous discipline. My German apartment is twice that size. How I furnish the rooms is entirely up to me. I am tempted to call Ikea for a free consultation.

*

The rules that govern a ger are invisible to the eye, but it's easy to appreciate its practical design.

In wooded areas settlers traditionally built their shelters around conifer trees, but long expeditions on the open steppe necessitated something more transportable. The Mongolian nomads and other nomadic peoples from Central Asia, southern Siberia and north of the Great Wall made their first tents from wooden stakes arranged in a circle and draped with furs.

Now, as then, the latticed walls of the ger are made from willow or similarly flexible wood. The design arose from the nomads' desire for greater freedom inside the tent and for protection against the tearing wind on the steppe. There is no need for nails; the circular walls consist of slats lashed together with leather bands. Each trellis collapses like an accordion, taking up very little space during the move.

Traditionally, the door faces south. I watched the sun rise every morning during my summer holidays on the land. The wooden doorway made up a rough picture frame through which the distant mountain greeted me in an ever-changing light. The landscape is uncluttered: mountains, the yellowish-green steppe beneath and the sky above, clouds scudding on the wind.

The felt awning is usually tacked up to allow a breeze to sweep along the floor and dissipate the heat, which can become unbearable. From inside the ger, you always look south. In colloquial Mongolian no distinction is made between left and east, right and west: for each direction there is only one word.

In wintertime the awning extends to the ground. The three-centimetre felt has the insulating properties of a six-centimetre brick wall. Three or four layers of felt are fastened to the lattice walls when the cold sets in.

The stove at the centre of the ger provides an even heat. Nomadic families see their stoves as sacred. At wedding ceremonies the bride consents to marriage by lighting a fire, thereby calling a new family into being.

Two or three metres above the ground an aperture in the roof serves as a sundial. The slanting light dictates when to do chores such as milking or herding. A nomad knows exactly where the shadow will fall at a particular time of day, depending on the season. During filming, our plans for the next day were always determined at bedtime by the constellations of the summer sky. If the stars appeared to touch the stove-pipe, the sun was on its way.

I hear the doorbell: a delivery.

No one shouts a warning about 'holding the dog', the customary Mongolian announcement of a visitor's approach. I hear the elevator whirr into action. The stranger does not clear his throat or stamp his feet to avoid the potential embarrassment of surprising his host.

A ger can offer no privacy to couples with children, which

is why our songs speak of the steppe as a place where lovers meet: 'Night-time is light ashamed of love'.

The elevator slides open. I peer through the spy-hole, turn the key in the door and unfasten the safety chain. A piece of home has arrived. I position the gaily painted, orange wooden table in my living room. A new place of honour.

21

The pack animals are ready to go. Tethered to the spot, they wait by the pen where the smaller animals are kept. The strongest bulls in the herd test their strength against each other. Lowering their horns, the half-wild yaks glare proudly at one another. Their breath hangs heavy in the fresh morning air.

The sun remains hidden behind the mountains but its rays steal into the valley. Batchuluun has arranged the ox-carts in a circle around the ger. The sky above the stove-pipe is clear of smoke. Two cranes clean their plumage in the little lake beside the camp.

The night was over quickly. Buena unties the cords of braided yak hair that run round the outside of the ger. Little is said as she and her husband dismantle the tent. Their movements are finely attuned, like a choreographed dance. The canvas peels away from the walls, pulled by one set of hands from the right of the door and another from the left. Their paths meet at the rear of the ger and the canvas is laid on the grass. Two sets of hands reach up for the felt awning and go their separate ways until the circuit is complete. A single tug, and the felt falls to the ground. The bare wooden skeleton reveals the ger's interior. Everything the family owns has been parcelled up and is lying in the open.

Batbayar senses that today is a special occasion. He romps excitedly among the family's belongings, now wrapped in blankets and cloth. Meanwhile, his sisters are filling a small sack with dried strips of cheese. Nansaa spies Zochor through the latticed wall. Tethered to a stick, he can only watch as his shade is dismantled piece by piece. The stream is beyond his reach.

Buena and Batchuluun have progressed to the roof. One by one the poles are detached from the centre, leaving Batchuluun, arms outstretched, bearing the weight of the roof ring. He lowers it slowly to the ground.

Buena takes hold of the window from the other side of the wall. At the last minute, when the caravan is ready and waiting, this prized possession will be laid on top of the leading cart.

The felt-lined carts are gradually loaded with belongings. The whole family is involved in the process. Carrying as much as she can manage, Nansalmaa offloads the goods to her father, who ties the packages together and straps them to the cart. Buena heaves the clothes chest on to the cart while Nansaa rolls up the rug. Dishes, buckets and milk pails are stored on one cart; chests, beds and mirrors on the next. Knots must be fastened, ropes pulled taut and drawers strapped shut. The door, formerly the boundary between inside and outside, stands forlornly on the grass.

Batbayar is tending the sheep. No sooner have the animals formed a huddle than Batbayar throws pebbles at them and they scatter.

'Let's get this dung cleared up now,' Buena tells the girls.

A short distance from camp Batchuluun lights a fire to burn the debris. Nansaa spots the green ladle beside him and scoops it up.

Buena chases after her son: 'What would I do without you, my little herdsman?'

Batbayar is relishing the novelty of playing undisturbed. He kicks out at Buena as she carries him to the cart. His screams ring out. The dung basket has been fastened to the cart and will serve as his playpen during the ride.

Buena calls to her eldest daughter. 'Nansaa, I need you to look after your brother for me!'

Nansaa abandons the ladle by the stream and runs over to Batbayar who continues to grouse. His new pink dog, with whom he shares the basket, is no longer so engrossing now its batteries have run down. Batbayar lets out another shriek. He wants to get out.

Batchuluun harnesses the animals and lines up the seven carts. Nansaa leaves her brother and sneaks through the caravan to Zochor. The green plastic ladle is full of water from the stream. Zochor refuses to touch it. Nansaa ruffles the fur around his neck and he nestles in to her. She lifts his left ear and whispers something inside.

'We thank you, O beautiful land of Khangai,' declaims Batchuluun, 'for permitting us to spend the summer here.' Buena tosses spoonfuls of milk over the three large rocks placed by her husband on the former site of the stove. The stones represent the hearth that burned there for months and the eternal unity of the family: father, mother and child. Finally she sprinkles milk on the horses' stirrups and the wheels of each cart.

'We shall return.'

Batchuluun makes one last check on the ropes and inspects the leather straps that hold the caravan together. Buena is already on horseback, rounding up the errant sheep and goats along the stream. On Batchuluun's signal the caravan sets off. The wheels roll forwards with a squeal. Nansaa springs on to the back of the final carriage.

The departure brings a shift in language. 'Höög, höög, hög, hög,' calls Batchuluun, spurring on the yak-bulls. 'Tschu,' Buena encourages her horse, and kicks it gently. She raises her voice: 'Tschaa, tscha, tscha!' It takes a constant effort to keep the flock moving at the head of the procession.

Slowly the caravan pulls away from camp. Two circular depressions in the steppe are the only signs that a family once lived there. The grass is yellow and dry where the ger and the banag stood.

The journey is long. The yaks have slowed their pace. Their hooves move in harmony, but the undulating terrain saps their strength. The heat is draining.

Nansalmaa, exhausted by the effort of moving camp, has been lulled to sleep by the lurching cart. When she first lay back, she was shaded by a wool sack. Now the sun beats down on her face. Nansaa is perched to the rear of the final carriage, next to her father's securely tethered motorcycle. She has her back to the caravan and watches as the mountains and valleys merge into a haze.

The carts cross the modon guur, a rickety wooden bridge. There was a time when Nansaa worried that the bridge might not hold them. Her father used to assure her that the planks would be repaired, but they find themselves sidestepping the same old holes. Nansaa's fears seem unimportant to her now.

The caravan jolts over the bumpy track, wending its way among the grass-covered hills. All at once Nansaa spots a bright flash of colour on the ground. She jumps down and grabs the long strip of material.

'What are you doing, Nansaa?' shouts Buena, struggling to close the growing distance between the yaks and the flock. 'Get back on the cart!'

'I found a sash, Mother!' Nansaa waves the fabric in the air.

Buena instantly recognises Batbayar's belt. Tugging sharply on the reins, she canters to the head of the caravan and draws herself up in the saddle to peer inside the basket.

'Batchuluun, stop the cart!' She dismounts in a leap and snatches the lid from the basket, a look of panic on her face. 'Where's my boy?' she shouts.

Nansalmaa wakes with a start. 'Mother? What's wrong?' Buena continues to shout. Batchuluun stands in his stirrups and brings the caravan to a halt. She scours the carriages frantically. Batbayar is not there.

Nansaa races desperately after her mother who is running madly in the direction of the camp.

22

Batchuluun turns back, setting off at a gallop. His goal is an empty point in the distance. They have travelled a long way. His eighteen-month-old son could be lying anywhere. What if his fears are confirmed? Where is Batbayar?

Despite the horse's speed, Batchuluun would almost prefer to run. His son is missing. He needs to keep hoping, keep hurrying. He cracks the whip, even though the horse can go no faster. Its hoofs clatter across the rickety bridge. The cracks between the planks look vast. If Batchuluun is to find his son, he hopes it won't be here. Not daring to look over the sides, he crosses the bridge as the Suman Gol roars greedily beneath him, dark and cold.

His saddle slips precariously to one side. Batchuluun responds immediately, shifting his weight in the stirrups and regaining his balance just in time. He should stop and tighten the girth straps. The horse was full when he saddled it that morning, but the long and strenuous journey has taken its toll and the saddle sits loosely on its lean form. His son is in danger; there is no time to stop. Dark spots fleck the sky on the horizon. For the first time the ruggedness of the landscape oppresses him. He races on. There is nothing idle about the scavengers' movements overhead; they are circling intently.

A hill looms up, then another, obliterating his view. As he bears down on the campsite he sees the birds more clearly: vultures. They get bigger and bigger. The familiar valley opens before him. He tugs on the reins and feels a momentary flood of relief: the vultures are feasting on the carcasses of the sheep that he took to the lake.

The horse wheels round; he had forgotten to slacken the reins. Batchuluun's heart is in his mouth. Something is moving by the lake. He tries to focus, but his eyes brim with water. Shouting frantically he gallops down the escarpment. He has spotted his son.

The vultures queue up in hierarchical order, feeding on the

sheep. Batbayar totters towards them. The grey birds, taller than the child, hack at the bones with their long curved beaks.

'My boy, my boy!' shouts Batchuluun. Unable to hear him, the child stumbles on. It seems to Batchuluun that the horse has stopped moving. By now the saddle is hanging around its neck, but he pays no attention. A vulture fixes Batbayar with its hostile stare, its features pale as a death mask. The horse reaches the marshy shoreline and slows its pace.

Batchuluun leaps to the ground, brandishing his arms. A swathe of water stretches in front of him. He watches powerlessly as his son, separated from him by the lake, walks straight towards the danger.

A flurry of beating wings, a mass of dark shadow and a bark, then squawking and shrieking in the frenzy for fresh meat.

The dark mass of bodies lifts before Batchuluun's eyes. A white ball of fluff chases them, snapping and barking. It is Nansaa's dog.

Batchuluun snaps out of his paralysis and shoos the birds higher into the sky. He rushes to the far side of the lake. A lone dark bird, hunched and plump, advances along the bank, hobbling on demonic claws. Its powerful wings drag behind it; its belly too heavy to fly.

Batchuluun gathers his son in his arms and holds the smeared face in his hands. The sound of the child's wails is reassuring and he presses his head to his ear. He closes his eyes and hears the dog's barks. Zochor has sent the last of the scavengers into the sky. Batchuluun lowers his son.

'Gölög, gölög,' he beckons. His voice sounds raw and cracked. The dog stops, tail between its legs, eyeing him suspiciously. 'Zochor, Zochor!' Batchuluun extends his hand towards him. Nervously, the little dog slinks closer. Trailing around his neck is the rope and with it, the upturned post. It must have taken enormous effort to wrest it from the ground. Batchuluun lets the dog sniff his fingers. He unties the knot that he had used to bind him that morning.

Batchuluun rides across the steppe, blue skies above, green grass below, carrying his son. The dog follows behind. It is a long way to the caravan. Batchuluun spurs his horse to a gallop.

Glossary

Age ceremony Annual birthday celebrations are slowly catching on in Mongolia, especially in the cities. Traditionally, a child's life started when his or her braids were cut off during the hair cutting rite. After that, anniversaries were only celebrated once a person reached the age of sixty. The festivities took place on major birthdays only and were an expression of a culture that venerates age.

Archi Milk vodka. Made by distilling fermented milk in handmade wooden casks.

Batbayar Most Mongolian names have a meaning. 'Bat' means solid or robust; 'bayar' means festival. Since most names are multisyllabic, they tend to be abbreviated for everyday use, hence 'Batbayar' becomes 'Bagy'.

Deel Traditional dress of the Mongolian nomad. A robe-like garment made of materials such as cotton, silk or cashmere and lined with fur or pelts in the winter.

Emee Mongolian for 'grandmother'. Terms denoting kinship can also be used for trusted persons outside the family unit.

Ger Felt-clad wooden tent traditionally used by the nomads of Central Asia. The circular frame is easy to put up, take down and transport. The ger resembles the felt-covered dwelling structure of the 'yurt', derived from the Turkic.

Gölög Mongolian for 'whelp'.

Khangai Mountains Mountain range in the heart of Mongolia. The ancestral homeland of the Mongolian people lies between the Khangai and the Khentei ranges.

Milk tea A Mongolian favourite. The green tea is prepared with the boiled milk of goats, sheep, cows, yak or, in desert areas, camels. The drink is laced with salt. Depending on the region, other ingredients such as dried meat, rice, flour, green leaves or curds may be added.

Milk vodka See 'archi'.

Mongolian Altai Mountain range in western Mongolia famed for its mineral resources, including gold, silver, copper and iron.

Naadam festival National day celebrations commemorating Mongolia's liberation from the Chinese in 1921. Wrestling, horse racing and archery competitions are held over three days in mid-July.

'Nearly tripped and died' Death is an abiding presence in the language and culture of Mongolia and is found at the heart of many proverbs and sayings, for instance: 'There is no guarantee that you will see the sun tomorrow but there are thousands of ways to die'.

New Year Celebrated in spring, according to the lunar calendar.

Om mani padme hum Buddhist mantra. Om = man, mani = jewel, padme = lotus flower, hum = Buddha: 'Let each man be a jewel on a lotus flower like Buddha.' According to Buddhist teaching, our minds are blighted by hatred, greed and ignorance. Earthly life is full of grime and suffering and humans alone have the potential to transcend the mire. When Buddha attained enlightenment, he rose through the swamp and blossomed like a lotus flower.

Prayer beads The beads are held in the right hand. With each spoken mantra, a bead is pushed through the fingers towards the palm. There are 108 beads, with a pendant marking the beginning and end of the chain.

Roof ring The roof ring consists of a hoop of wood at the apex of the roof. The roof poles slot into the ring. It can be opened to let in light and air and to release smoke.

Snuff Traditionally exchanged as part of the greeting ritual. Snuff bottles come in various sizes and are made of ebony, silver or gemstones. The coral stopper comes with a miniature silver or gold spoon.

Sum An administrative subdivision. The country is divided into 340 somon, with at least ten somon to every province or aimag. Mongolia has twenty-one aimags.

Suman Gol River in the Tariat district that flows through a lava gorge measuring twenty to thirty metres deep.

Tschaak Nansaa says 'tschaak, tschaak, tschaak' as she herds the sheep. Batchuluun drives the yak with shouts of 'höög, höög, hög, hög', while Buena spurs on her horse by calling 'tschu'. The nomads have a special language for communicating with their livestock, using set noises for each variety of animal. Different sounds are used to instruct a goat to stop or a sheep to start moving and so forth.

Tugrik Unit of currency. 1 tugrik = 100 mungo.

Ulaanbaatar Capital of Mongolia, the eighteenth largest country in the world. Mongolia is four times the size of Germany and covers an area of 1.5 million square kilometres. Some 800,000 of its 2.5 million inhabitants live in the capital. The western spelling of Ulaanbaatar is 'Ulan Bator'. The name translates as 'red hero'. Until 1924 the city was called Örgo, meaning 'noble ger'. It was incorrectly translated as 'Urga', meaning lasso on the end of a pole.

Winter camp Camp used by nomadic families during the winter. Winter camps are usually passed from generation to generation. Each camp is shared with at least two other families. No livestock is kept at the camp from spring to autumn in order to spare the pastures.

Acknowledgements

We are very grateful to the Batchuluuns, Batbayar Davgadori, the Reichs, the film crew, Bettina Feldweg and the Munich Academy of Television and Film for giving us their trust and their support.

Byamba & Lisa

Photographs are from the filming of *The Cave of the Yellow Dog*, directed by Byambasuren Davaa and starring Batchuluun Urjindorj, Buyandulam Daramdadi Batchuluun, Nansaa Batchuluun, Nansalmaa Batchuluun and Batbayar Batchuluun. A Schesch production in association with the Munich Academy of Television and Film. Producer: Stephan Schesch, Associate Producer: Luethje & Schneider Filmproduktion, Stills: Monika Höfler, Director of Photography: Daniel Schönauer. Supported by the German Federal Film Board, the Film Commission Bavaria and the Federal Commissioner for Cultural and Media Affairs.